ERDY MCHENRY ARCHITECTURE – TWENTY YEARS

TABLE OF CONTENTS

FOREWORD

1001 – Southern Poverty Law Center
1003 – My Brother's Keeper
1009 – Suburban Cable
1013 – Walnut Street Lofts
1021 – All Pro Landscaping
1034 – Church of St. Aloysius
1060 – Penn Cafe and Collaboratory
1071 – The Piazza at Schmidt's Commons
1073 – Coatesville Redevelopment
1077 – Avenue North
1093 – Cunningham Piano Building
1097 – The Radian
1098 – Independence Mall Café
1104 – 3 Crescent Drive
1107 – Millennium Hall
1116 – Vertical Screen
1118 – Lumen-Air House
1120 – Cornell University Teaching Dairy Barn
1121 – Intermodal Transportation Center
1124 – 330 Cooper Street
1126 – Syracuse Law College Housing
1133 – University of Pennsylvania Stuart Weitzman School of Design
1135 – Convention Center Parking Facility
1137 – Courtyard Marriott at The Philadelphia Navy Yard
1142 – Evo & Cira Green
1151 – 6 Great Valley Parkway
1154 – Woodlands at Arborcrest
1159 – Holly Pointe Commons
1165 – Lumpkin's Jail Interpretive Center
1177 – Axalta Global Innovation Center
1178 – LIV Birmingham
1179 – Bank Barn
1181 – City Twin
1182 – Hostel CO-OP
1188 – Trestle Park
1190 – Franklin County Extension
1192 – Neptune Campus West

ACKNOWLEDGMENTS

INDEX

EPILOGUE

Foreword

In 2006, the U.S. National Park Service commissioned Erdy McHenry Architecture to design retail kiosks for Independence National Historic Park in Center City Philadelphia. The park had been conceived in the 1940s and 1950s as a Cold War shrine to American democracy. With the two-block Independence Mall, the architecture firm Harbeson, Howe, Livingston & Larson designed, as Lewis Mumford wrote in the New Yorker, "a handsome frame for the old picture" of Independence Hall and the other modest Georgian buildings of the American Revolution and early republic. Through aggressive demolition the architects framed out the layers of public commercial life that had collected there for two centuries, leaving an overly grand, uninhabited, and monolithic approach to Independence Hall, a somber shrine rather than an animated district in the center of a dynamic city.

At the time Scott Erdy and David McHenry's firm received the commission from the Park Service, they had been developing, testing, and revising ideas for a project called the Piazza, located a few miles away, in Northern Liberties, an equally old section of the city with a rich and tangible history of invention and defiance. Artists, makers, and dreamers had been moving into the mixed-race neighborhood since the 1970s, creating a social world that most urban observers, even by the late-1990s, had imagined to be a thing of the past, or of the fringe. In an increasingly suburban, stiffly zoned, and frustratingly atomized nation, urban space was to be feared by the vast proportion of Americans who felt, no differently from the original designers of Independence Mall, that cities had to be cleansed.

From the beginning, Erdy McHenry's practice focused heavily on the foundational questions that would guide each project. "The basis of our engagement with any project is in the design of the approach," says McHenry, of a process that necessitates listening and observing closely and that has resulted over the last twenty years in the firm's transformational body of work, celebrated in this monograph. Muscular in form and exactingly sensitive to context, Erdy McHenry's approach makes it a true successor of the 20th century Philadelphia School of Architecture, and, as the organizers of a 2017 exhibit at the University of Pennsylvania and architecture critic Inga Saffron have noted, the harbinger of a 21st century version.

Since the firm's earliest commission in 1999 for the Southern Poverty Law Center in Montgomery Alabama through to their proposed designs for LIV Birmingham in England. Erdy McHenry's buildings have become living elements of place, history guides, and mirrors on our distinctly self-aware urban age—what I call an architecture for seeing.

This doesn't mean their work is somehow invisible, as if to mimic or blend in. The opposite is true of design that responds fiercely to need—what is obvious and intrinsic and what is hidden and invisible. By helping clients, neighbors, inhabitants, tenants, and the casual observer to find themselves in the material history of place, Erdy and McHenry are indeed architects of far and near vision, and both at once.

In getting to work on the Piazza, Scott and David found themselves confronted with a narrative that ran counter to the vision of the original Independence Mall designers, of an unruly, self-creating neighborhood that had built its own park on the grounds of a 19th century tannery and where the economy emerged from messy communal life. The narrative of self-creation was being inscribed on neighborhood spaces and in real time reified by its authors, the residents themselves; social, self-aware, and inspired by earlier generations of inhabitants, at the turn of the 21st century in Northern Liberties and a handful of other neighborhoods across the country a new form of urban life was being born. "We try to embrace the conditions in a direct way," says Erdy, elaborating on the firm's design approach. Through this sensitivity they transformed the Piazza from a one-dimensional concept proposed by the client to a multi-layered stage for public life, and came to understand, far before most of us, that the future of cities was going to be consciously and intentionally social and experiential. In this sense, starting with the Piazza and followed particularly by the Independence Mall Cafe, Radian, Millennium Hall, 330 Cooper Street, and Evo/Cira Green, buildings that direct their users to see themselves publicly performing their own version of city life, Erdy McHenry Architecture anticipated the Instagram age.

The National Park Service chose the landscape architecture firm Olin to fix the mistakes of the original Independence Mall design. Intimate spaces would be created where actors could engage the visitor in the history underfoot, a visual connection would be established between the National Constitution Center and Independence Hall, and retail kiosks would provide amenities.

The instinct to inject commercial activity into the park marked a change in philosophy about American urban space, suggesting that it could once again be multi-dimensional, but Park Service officials lacked an understanding of urban dynamics. Moreover, the budget was too small to build multiple kiosks or to heat or cool them (perhaps budget constraints are the most common condition to be embraced by the architect). Erdy McHenry's solution, rather than multiple kiosks, was to build a single cafe that could open completely, loggia style, expanding the small footprint into the wider space of the park.

To longtime urban observers like me this felt like a revolutionary act (I had recently written an essay, "A Whole Lot of Meaning and Nothing To Do," on the sterility of urban public space). Erdy McHenry's refined design was slender and transparent and at the same time—employing corten steel and wood—rich and rooted, nothing like the new visitor's center, Liberty Bell pavilion, and bathrooms installed on Independence Mall, brick boxes decorated with useless Georgian and Federal flourishes.

I recall my own disbelief that the Park Service had accepted the design. It was most certainly a result of Scott and David's ability to discern financial and programmatic need and communicate that need back to the client in a humbly persuasive manner. The building had to be economically self-sufficient, and it had to deepen the visitor experience. Those were the stated needs, but the architects, I believe, ascertained something more: the urgency to express, through architecture, layers of time. The new cafe, after all, was a manifestation of the 21st century. And as a 21st century expression it had to do more than function. The cafe had to perform—because it does so with such refinement it remains for me a favorite Erdy McHenry design.

Inserted into an intimate garden above street level, the cafe clamps onto the wall of the parking garage under the park. Facing the gravesite of Benjamin Franklin it reminds us that public commercial life in the New World was a Franklin invention. Etched in the glass walls of the building on the park and street sides, CAFE (in Erdy McHenry's signature Microgramma font) becomes a legible gesture of the 21st century in a neighborhood that once thrilled with painted signs and the voices of hucksters, hustlers, and market vendors. This is the point of architecture, says Erdy. "All places, (cities in particular)

are a tapestry of memory deposited over time. The size, shape, and materiality of our buildings express this memory and intention, and lay bare the cultural expression of place. We are a contemporary architectural practice that approaches each project as 'the second architect,' interpreting the history of a site, place, and purpose."

Just as the Independence Mall cafe grips the retaining wall above the street, Evo, a finely detailed 33-story residential tower, bolts onto the wall that suspends the city street above the former Pennsylvania Railroad tracks heading in and out of 30th Street Station. These installations reflect Erdy's notion of the second architect, the architecture attaching itself as lens, active interpreter, and guide.

Each of them installed on constrained sites defined by conflicted social, architectural, historical, and emotional contexts, the Independence Mall Cafe, the Piazza, Avenue North, Radian, Millennium Hall, 330 Cooper Street, and Evo pull back, turn, or suspend above to reveal "the cultural expression of place" as an accumulation of time. As actions, the pulling back, turning, and suspending above—buildings performing!—are themselves legible, revealing a contemporary awareness and embrace of multiple eras at once. This is truly an architecture for seeing. Such legibility brings the city experience to life, says McHenry. "It promotes inquiry and investigation, which by definition are active interactions with the object and the context rather than simply passive observations."

From the beginning, Scott Erdy and David McHenry have wanted their work to be absorbed into place as dynamic elements. The Southern Poverty Law Center building in Montgomery Alabama, for example, would become part of a history of place already underway—and deepen our experience of it going forward. In this way their work masterfully

illustrates a concept I've long considered in my writing, that place is a product of the intersection of the metaphysical (ideals and ideas, histories and memories) and the physical (streets and buildings, materials and forms). This is the grand performance of Erdy McHenry Architecture.

Around the time Erdy McHenry started working on the Southern Poverty Law Center project, I solicited a bid from Scott and David on behalf of the Enterprise Center, where I worked, for a building to house second-stage start-ups. During their presentation they explained the name of their fledgling firm. "We aren't Erdy McHenry Architects," they said. "We are Erdy McHenry Architecture. It's the work that matters, not us." It's the work that demands the architect to be humble and listen—and to know when and how to reframe the question. My colleagues and I were so struck by this notion, as well as Scott and David's genuine curiosity and desire to make buildings of lasting power, that we hired them almost immediately. So began a long affection. I hope the reader will examine the dozens of projects that follow this foreword with an equal sense of wonder and appreciation.

Twenty years since I got to know them and their work I've been lucky enough to watch Erdy McHenry's architecture transform the city where I live, and not with any uniform style. From the Independence Mall Cafe to the Axalta Global Innovation Center what's legible, and alive in the cityscape, is their thinking—about the purpose of architecture and the stories it allows us to tell about ourselves as we negotiate time and space. This is a great personal benefit, one I imagine will be shared with many people in the coming decades as Erdy McHenry's architecture awakens all kinds of messy places across the globe.

Nathaniel Popkin
Fall 2020

1091
SOUTHERN POVERTY LAW CENTER
MONTGOMERY, AL

SOUTHERN POVERTY LAW CENTER
1999-2001

By the late 1960s, the civil rights movement had ushered in the promise of racial equality as changes in federal law and decisions by the U.S. Supreme Court put an end to Jim Crow segregation. New legislation was slow to bring about the fundamental changes needed in the South; in part because few lawyers were willing to take controversial cases to test these new civil rights laws. A selfless decision by two southern lawyers to provide a voice for the disenfranchised led to the founding of the Southern Poverty Law Center. Distinguished by its nearly half-century legacy of fighting hate, teaching tolerance, and seeking justice for victims denied by criminal courts, the Center itself became the victim of hate when their offices were firebombed by Klansmen just before 4 AM on an otherwise quiet Sunday morning.

Undeterred, the Center was up and running in a matter of days on folding tables in an old warehouse. In the years that followed, the center reaffirmed its place and purpose by sponsoring the Civil Rights Memorial, created by Maya Lin, designer of the Vietnam Veterans Memorial, at its office in Montgomery. Ultimately, a new headquarters for SPLC was commisioined on hallowed ground between the Dexter Avenue Baptist Church, where Dr. Martin Luther King, Jr. started his public preaching and the site of the memorial honoring those who gave their lives in the struggle for civil rights. This context of place and memory weighed heavily as Erdy McHenry embarked on giving form to the mission of the Southern Poverty Law Center.

Respectful of its context, the new headquarters sets back from the street, both to afford precinct to the memorial and to facilitate the defensible space objectives in response to the inevitable social construct of hate. In a singular gesture, the east end of the building cleaves itself apart and rises up in deference to the axis connecting the historical King Church, where the civil right movement established its momentum, with the contemporary memorial honoring the selfless sacrifice of many who gave their last full measure of devotion in support of the cause.

The functional organization and formal massing of the building is arranged with the primary workspace oriented to the north with a full height curtain wall to create a column-free daylit workplace recalling the energy of the organization from the days of the folding tables in the warehouse and fostering a renewed culture of interaction among lawyers and staff, whose workspace had previously been segregated by hard-wall offices. Facing south, the building takes on a more solid massing in deference to the memorial. Two major apertures in the south façade contain double height reference libraries that provide inter-floor connectivity to support collaboration between the investigation, litigation, and education functions of the Center. Individuals come together in the libraries to advance the mission, while views through the window to the memorial provide a simple yet poignant reminder of the significance of their efforts.

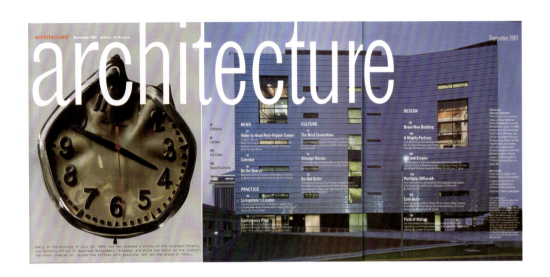

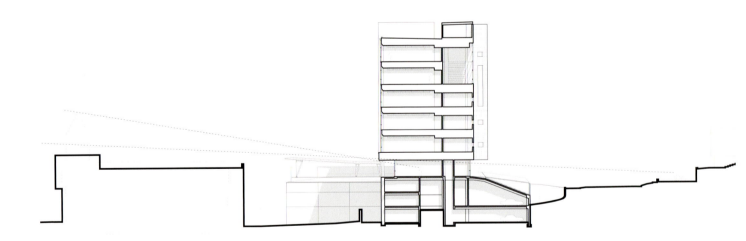

Site Section

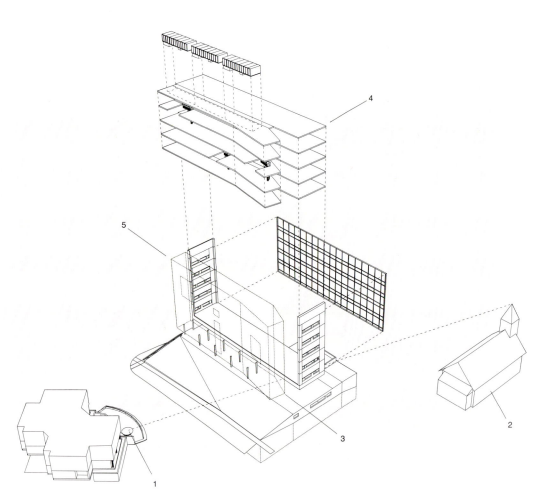

Powerful Sightlines: Diagrammatic Axon

The Civil Rights Memorial (1) by Maya Lin was built across from the Dexter Avenue Baptist Church (2) where Martin Luther King, Jr. began his public preaching. In a singular gesture, the east end of the building (3) cleaves itself apart and rises up in deference to the axis connecting to the historical King Church. The functional organization and formal massing of the building is arranged with the primary workspace oriented to the north (4). Facing south, the building takes on a more solid massing (5) in deference to the memorial.

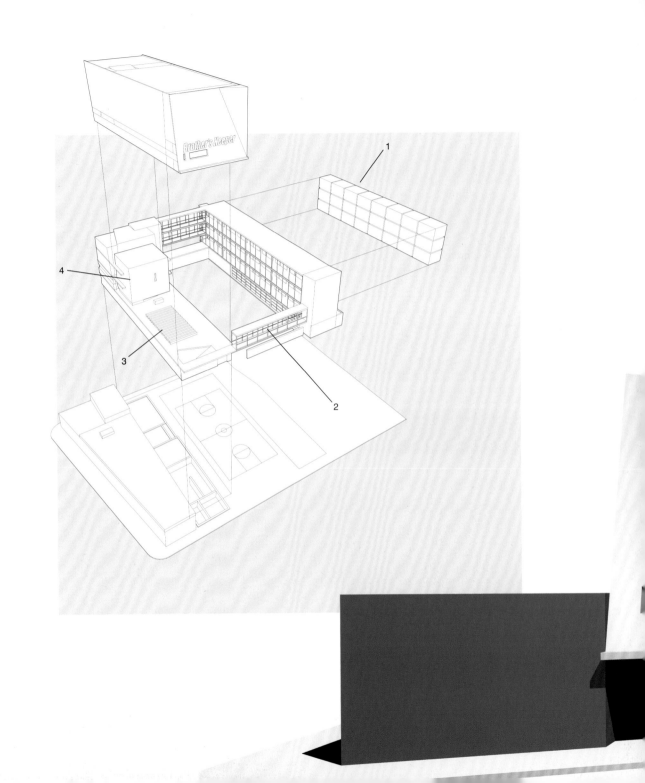

MY BROTHER'S KEEPER
CAMDEN, NJ

There is a marked discrepancy between the number of people who need addiction treatment in the United States and those who actually receive it. People go untreated for many reasons. They may be reluctant to seek treatment because they hold certain beliefs about it. They may not have insurance to cover the cost, or they may live in an area where treatment isn't available.

My Brother's Keeper stands in that breach offering faith based treatment for drug and alcohol addiction among other outreach services in the City of Camden regardless of the ability to pay. The men in the program reside in shared accommodations in a modest dormitory block (1), affording both solitude and support while going through the challenging process of rehabilitation. In the course of their treatment, they come together several times daily for prayer, fellowship, and instruction. Their journey to the chapel is visible to the outside world when they cross the courtyard bridge (2) that links the housing to the chapel. Because many of the residents in the program are pressured by their outside partners to leave the program early on in order to provide for their fledgling families, the bridge is clad in a translucent glass which allows only their silhouette to be visible to the outside. The chapel interior (3) is oriented toward a large granite-clad monolith (4) that contains the detoxification rooms where each resident must spend their first weeks fully abandoning their addiction. The men who come together each day for prayer and instruction sit in support of these newest members by facing this object in spiritual support and as a reminder of their own personal journey.

The monolith is bathed in natural light from an overhead cruciform skylight creating, with varying degrees of clarity, the only religious symbolism in the building.

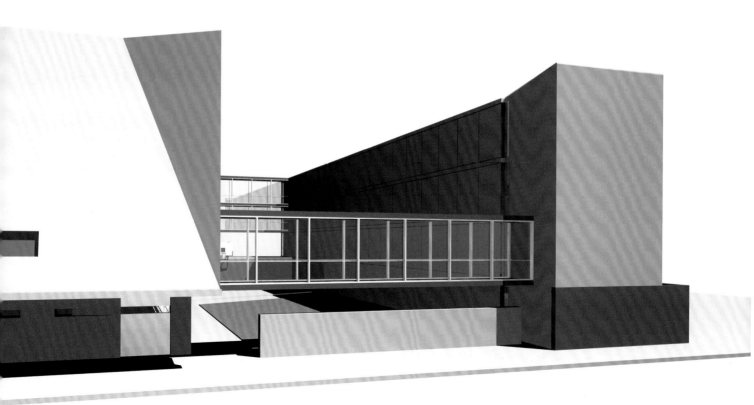

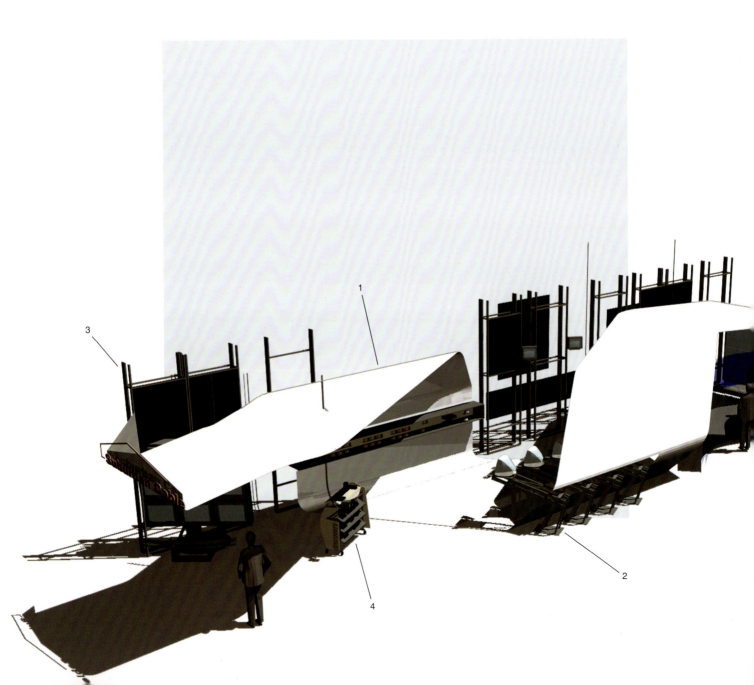

1999

SUBURBAN CABLE
PROTOTYPE

In 1999, Suburban Cable was at the forefront of cable TV's high speed internet access promoting cable modems with speeds somewhere in the 30 Mbps range.

The concept was somewhat foreign to most computer users but the upside to providers was huge. The notion of connectivity was a new concept to most of us so getting the public to embrace this new technology required more than media advertising and direct mail could offer. This retail prototype was envisioned as part customer service and part training center where the available technologies of the time could be compared side by side.

The Möbius strip (1) formally articulates Suburban's connection with its customers and the customer's ability to connect with the world across the ubiquitous continuum of digital communication. It also tied in Suburban's desire to achieve brand continuity across their broadening product/service offerings.

Internet access is facilitated in the Internet Café by computers (2) protruding through the Möbius strip on robust armatures that contrast the delicate hardware and the physical connections they support. Products and services are displayed in product galleries (3) embedded within the Möbius strip to engage the customer with the element of imagery in a tactile way. Similarly, the strip traverses the floor uninterrupted, crossing paths with the customer and connecting the two for a brief initial contact. Promotional material is presented on moveable carts (4) to add variety and flexibility to the presentation of the product offering. Pricing and other product information is presented on touch-screen LCD displays on the cart connected to the retail infrastructure through visible conduits that drop out of the ceiling grid.

Linked by the Möbius strip yet held in discrete containers, the diverse products and services are presented in a retail prototype strategy responsive to the initial challenge set out by the client.

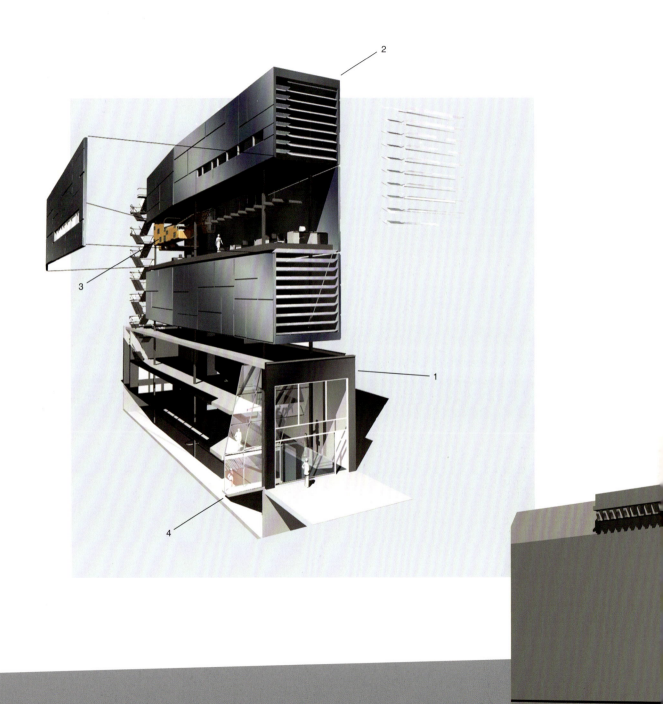

WALNUT STREET LOFTS
PHILADELPHIA, PA

An underutilized two-story structure (1) in a vibrant urban strip in Center City Philadelphia presents a challenging adaptive reuse opportunity: to leverage the embodied energy of an existing structure in support of an additive intervention that maximizes unused development potential (2). This feasibility study commissioned by Goldman Properties (of Soho and South Beach fame) seeks to explore new strategies and technologies which respond to and support the balance of work and family by creating a livable loft technologically and structurally supported by infrastructure. This equilibrium is achieved by the insertion of a workspace (3) which is visually segregated from the living space but functionally integrated into the interior environment and the larger urban context.

The overbuild needles through the existing structure emphasizing the different uses in both form and expression. The front wall is louvered to control the southern exposure while the north side opens to accept natural daylight for artist lofts or other live/work scenarios. This proposal also explores creative strategies to access natural light in a zero-lot-line condition while remaining compliant with applicable zoning and code restrictions and requirements. Multi-level retail (4) maximizes available frontage while maintaining convenient access.

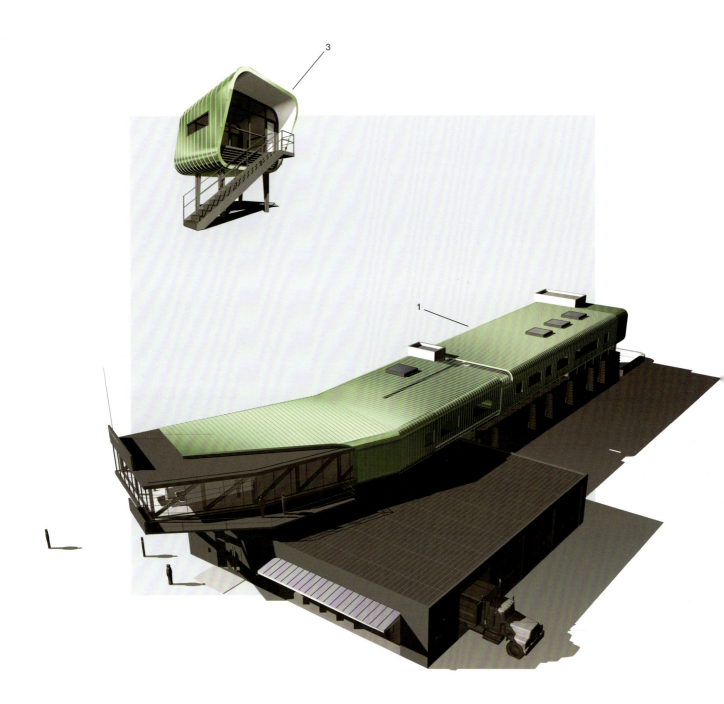

ALL PRO LANDSCAPING
HAINESPORT, NJ

All Pro Landscaping, a landscape construction, maintenance and irrigation contractor, purchased a 30-acre partially wooded parcel along a busy commercial highway in the southern part of New Jersey to consolidate its operations currently dispersed over several leased facilities.

The building (1) expresses the nature of the landscape operation and the cultural idiosyncrasies of the organization in its form and materials. Nestled deep in the site, the base (2) of the building utilizes materials typically employed in landscapes. An organic eruption of the ground plane forms the enclosure of the ground floor of the building, thus creating a plinth upon which the machine-like expression of the building's upper story positions itself. This juxtaposition expresses the relationship between the equipment and the landscape that is at the heart of the construction and maintenance operations of the organization. The Operations Building bends (3) to embrace foreground parterre elements and to screen views to the materials inventory beyond. The skin is torn back as a result of the stresses imposed by this bending, exposing the president's office (3) which is cantilevered over the road to provide a panoramic view of the yard, crews, and the remaining functional components of the operation.

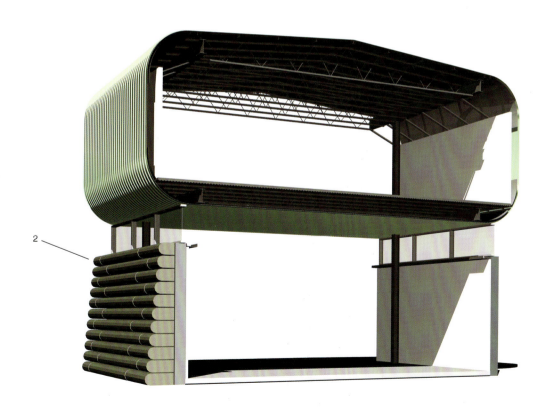

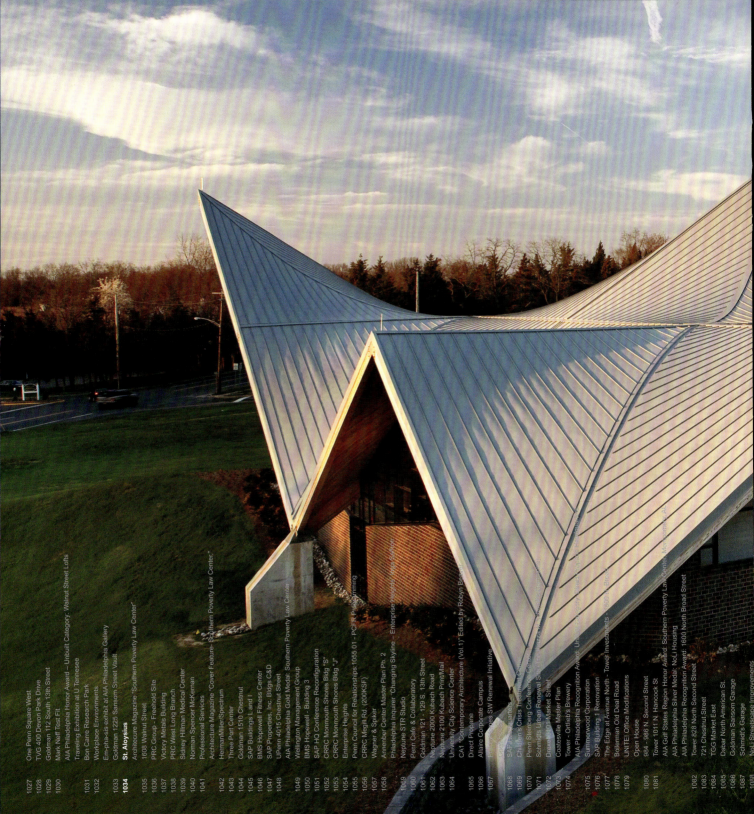

1027	One Penn Square West
1028	TVG 400 Devon Park Drive
1029	Goldman 112 South 13th Street
1030	Mark Net Test Fit
1031	AIA Philadelphia Honor Award – Unbuilt Category: Walnut Street Lofts Traveling Exhibition at U Tennessee
1032	Bon Carre Research Park
1033	Workplace Environments Em-pha-sis exhibit at AIA Philadelphia Gallery Goldman 1225 Sansom Street Vault
1034	**St. Aloysius**
1035	Architecture Magazine "Southern Poverty Law Center"
1036	1608 Walnut Street
1037	PRC Group - Freehold Site
1038	Victory Metals Building
1039	PRC West Long Branch
1040	Sidney Hillman Medical Center
1041	Norman Spencer McKernan Professional Services
1042	Architecture Magazine "Cover Feature – Southern Poverty Law Center."
1043	HermanMiller/Spectrum
1044	Three Port Center
1045	Goldman 1510 Chestnut
1046	SAP Buildings I and J
1047	BMS Hopewell Fitness Center
1048	SAP Properties, Inc. Bldgs C&D UPenn 4015 Chestnut Street
1049	AIA Philadelphia Gold Medal: Southern Poverty Law Center Wellington Management Group
1050	BMS Hopewell – Building 3
1051	SAP HQ Conference Reconfiguration
1052	CRRC Monmouth Shores Bldg "S"
1053	CRRC Monmouth Shores Bldg "J"
1054	Enterprise Heights
1055	Penn Council for Relationships 1055.01 – PCFR Programming
1056	CRRC Megill Rd. (200/KSF)
1057	Wagner & Spiker
1058	Annenber Center Master Plan Ph. 2 Philadelphia Inquirer "Changing Skyline – Enterprise Heights" Inga Saffron
1059	Neptune STR Studio
1060	Penn Cafe & Collaboratory
1061	Goldman 121 - 129 S. 13th Street
1062	Neptune 2000 Kubach Road
1063	Neptune 2100 Kubach Print/Mail
1064	University City Science Center CA1 "Contemporary Architecture (Vol. 1)" Edited by Robyn Beaver
1065	Direct Propane
1066	Allaire Corporate Campus
1067	Summerwood Corporation Jones SW Renewal Initiative
1068	SAP Fitness Center
1069	Children's Crisis Treatment Center
1070	Penn Steinberg Conference Center
1071	Schmidts Urban Renewal Strategy
1072	Drexel 30th Market Street
1073	Coatesville Master Plan
1074	Tower – Ortlieb's Brewery
1075	AIA Philadelphia Recognition Award: Southern Poverty Law Center, Montgomery AL
1076	Summerwood Corporation
1077	The Edge at Avenue North – Tower Investments – 1500 N. Broad Street
1078	Bollerman Old Deal Road
1079	UNITE! Office Modifications Open House
1080	984 - 986 N. Second Street
1081	Tower 1011 N. Hancock St. AIA Philadelphia Recognition Award: 1600 North Broad Street AIA Philadelphia Silver Medal: NoLi Housing
1082	Tower 828 North Second Street
1083	721 Chestnut Street
1084	TGG Market East
1085	Dabar North American St.
1086	Goldman Sansom Garage
1087	Schmidt's Garage

1034
CHURCH OF ST. ALOYSIUS
JACKSON, NJ

1096 — AIA Philadelphia Honor Award - Unbuilt Category: Schmidt's Garage
1097 — AIA Philadelphia Silver Medal: Coatesville Redevelopment
— Drexel Campus Master Plan
— The Radian
1098 — Drexel University LeBow College of Business
1099 — Philadelphia Inquirer "Hometown Modernists" EM Firm Profile
1100 — Independence Mall Café - IVCC Café
1101 — McNeil Residence - Chestnut Hill
1102 — NoLi Partners 915 N. Orianna
— Student Housing Solutions - Widener
— Arrow Screw Swim Club
1103 — AIA Philadelphia Honor Award - Built Category: NoLi Housing
1104 — Pennsylvania Ballet
1105 — 3 Crescent Drive - LPT
1106 — Grasso Holdings Pepper Bldg
1107 — Grasso Holdings - 2100 South St.
1108 — Millenium Hall - Drexel 34th Street Student Housing
1109 — NJNG Wyckoff Rd
— Syracuse School of Architecture Exhibit
— Project H.O.M.E.
1110 — Inland Post Office Annex Site
— Move to Orianna Street Offices
1111 — Rialto - Hancock Square - Building K "Office Egg" at Schmidt's
1112 — Tower State Office Bldg
1113 — AIA Pennsylvania Excellence in Design Honor Award - NoLi Housing
— AIA Philadelphia Honor Award - Unbuilt Category: 1316 Chestnut Street
— Philadelphia Water Department, Office of Watersheds, Best Stormwater Management Plan
— GBCA Construction Excellence Award: Best Design Built Project - Drexel University Residence Hall
1114 — CRRC Jumping Brook
— Bollerman Parkway Falls
1115 — Parkway Corp. 23rd & Market
1116 — Vertical Screen - Warminster
1117 — Michaels Development - Cooper Housing
— Architectural Record "Urban Multifamily Housing: Fringe Benefits" featuring "Open Spaces"
— Architectural Record "NoLi Housing"
1118 — Philadelphia Inquirer "Changing Skyline" - Adding Coffee to the Culture, Independence Mall Café
— Lumen-Air House - Syracuse - From The Ground Up
1119 — Open House
— Drexel Dining Terrace
— AIA National Housing Award: NoLi Housing
— AIA Philadelphia Honor Award: Built Category: Independence Mall Café
— AIA Montgomery Avenue Chapter Honorable Mention: Southern Poverty Law Center
— DBIA Pennsylvania Tri-State Region Design-Build Project Award: Drexel University Race Street Residence Hall
— GBCA Construction Excellence Award: Best Design Built Project - Drexel University Residence Hall
1120 — Cornell Teaching Dairy Barn
1121 — Syracuse Intermodal Trans Center
1122 — Goldman Café District Victory
— Lights of Liberty
— Metal Architecture Magazine "Divine Dwelling"
1123 — Synterra Pitts Broad & Spring Garden
1124 — 330 Cooper Street - MDC - CCIA Rutgers Housing Camden
1125 — Campus Living Villages
1126 — SU Law College Housing (Campus West)
— Enterprise Center
— Fertile Ground Exhibition
1127 — Mariana Bracetti Academy
— The New York Times "From Abandoned Brewery to Piazza, Philly-Style" by Fred Bernstein
— AIA Philadelphia Honor Award - Unbuilt Category: Lumen-Air House
— AIA Philadelphia Honor Award - Built Category: The Piazza at Schmidt's
— AIA Philadelphia Merit Award - Built Category: The Radian
— Metal Construction Association President's Award: Roofing: St. Aloysius of Gonzaga Church
— Metal Architecture Magazine, Metal Roofing Award, St. Aloysius Church, Jackson, NJ
— McGraw Hill Mid-Atlantic Construction Award of Merit Higher Education/Drexel University Millennium Hall, Philadelphia
— McGraw Hill New York Construction's Best of 2009 Project of the Year Worship: The Church of St. Aloysius-Jackson, N.J.
— McGraw Hill New York Construction's Best of 2009 Judges' Award Best Architectural Design – The Church of St. Aloysius-Jackson, N.J.
— GBCA Construction Excellence Award: Best Design Built Project - Drexel University Residence Hall
— Best Overall Design Build Project: PA Region – Drexel University Race Street Residence Hall
— Philadelphia Inquirer "City's Green Groundbreakers" (Firm Profile) by S. Smith
1128 — University of the Arts
1129 — PPMC M.O.B./Surgery Center
— Ministry & Liturgy "St. Aloysius, A Tent for a Pilgrim People." by G. Scott Shaffer
1130 — Goldman - Newark City
— Open House
1131 — Railroad Museum of PA (DGS)
1132 — East Baltimore Community School

CHURCH OF ST. ALOYSIUS
2005-2009

The design of the Church of St. Aloysius began with the design team embarking on a journey of exploration and research with the pastor and the parishioners.

Aloysius Gonzaga was the firstborn in a powerful Italian noble family, one that was deeply involved in the ongoing business of dealing and double-dealing, treachery, and betrayal that marked the political life of the time. At the age of eight he served in the court of Grand Duke Francesco I de' Medici. Despite his father's plans for him, this was not the life Aloysius imagined for himself. He was drawn to a life of piety, sacrifice, and service.

When Aloysius was 18, he joined the Jesuits. In 1591, then in his fourth year of theological studies, a famine and pestilence broke out in Italy. Though in delicate health, he devoted himself to the care of the sick. Aloysius had four special devotions that guided his ministry and brought comfort and hope to those he served. The first of these was the devotion to the Blessed Sacrament of the Altar. A second favorite devotion of the Saint was that to the Passion of Our Lord. His third devotion was his ardent love of Our Lady. Lastly, Aloysius had a special devotion to the holy choir of Angels.

The Catholic Community of Saint Aloysius in Jackson, New Jersey was growing, and the prospect of building a new church presented the opportunity to better understand its patron saint and to commit themselves to the example of service and piety that guided his ministry.

The odyssey of research and discovery we shared with the pastor and parishioners led to two significant conceptual explorations that gave form to the design of this church. The delicate soaring roof lines evoke the concept of simple worship, recalling the nomadic roots of God's journeying people "Re-pitching the tent" in a liturgical action that acknowledges that this faith community has not arrived, but is in transit, discovering God not at the end of the journey but in the journeying. At the foundation of his spiritual journey, Saint Aloysius committed himself to four simple devotions - Blessed Sacrament, Passion of Our Lord, Love of Our Lady, and Choir of Angels. These devotions are memorialized as individual chapels within the church coincide with the four large concrete buttresses that anchor the hyperbolic paraboloid wood roof shell above, uniting the congregation for worship beneath its fluid lines akin to those of a fabric tent.

The transparency of the glazed clerestory between the earthly mass of the anchoring chapels and the celestial expression of the tent above fills the sanctuary with light symbolizing God's presence at the communal celebration of the Mass. The entry sequence is in concert with the social implications of gathering for worship. The main entry dictates a singular approach through a series of increasingly intimate spaces preparing congregants for worship in communion with their fellow parishioners. Individuals become one with each other as they are reoriented to the altar and renew their baptismal commitment by anointing themselves with holy water from the same baptismal font used for Christian initiation rites.

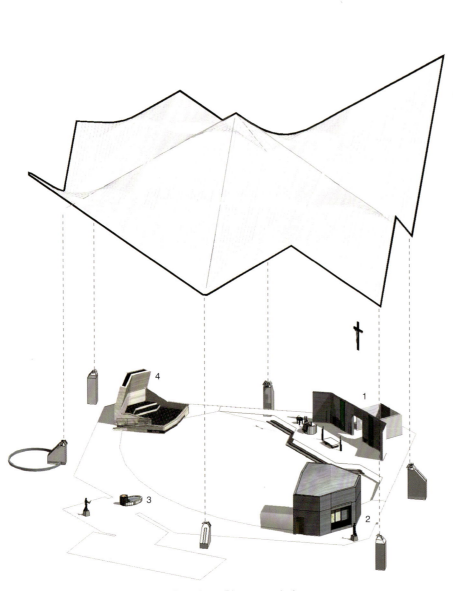

Four Devotions: Diagrammatic Axon

Careful consideration was given to the sacraments and their adjacencies: (1) Blessed Sacrament, (2) The Love of our Lady, (3) The Passion of Our Lord, (4) The Choir of Angels. Also considered was the orientation of the altar and the daily chapel to the baptismal font at the entry to the Sanctuary. The floating roof structure is metaphorically grounded by the four devotions whose locations provide the foundation to both the building and to this faithful congregation.

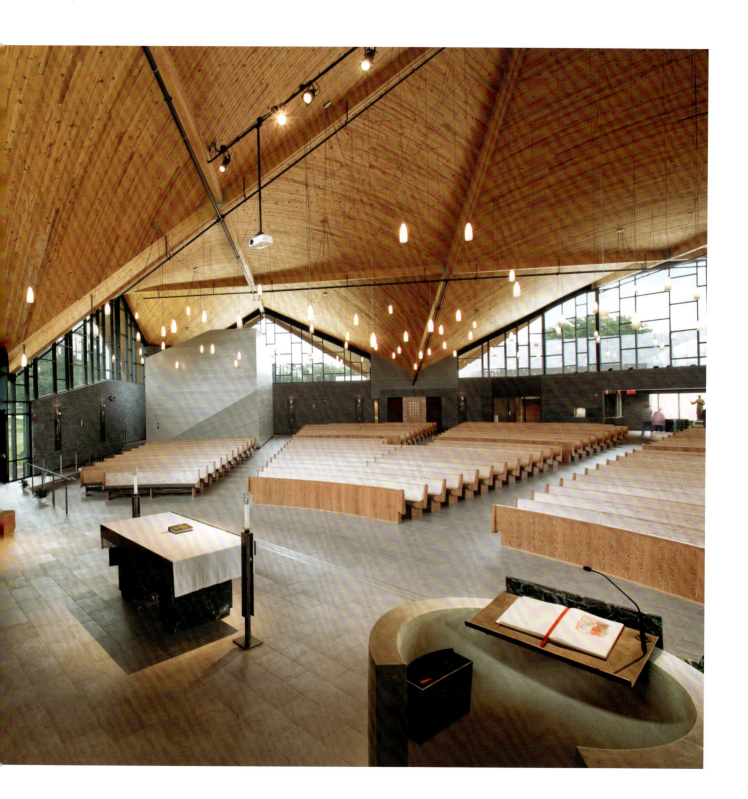

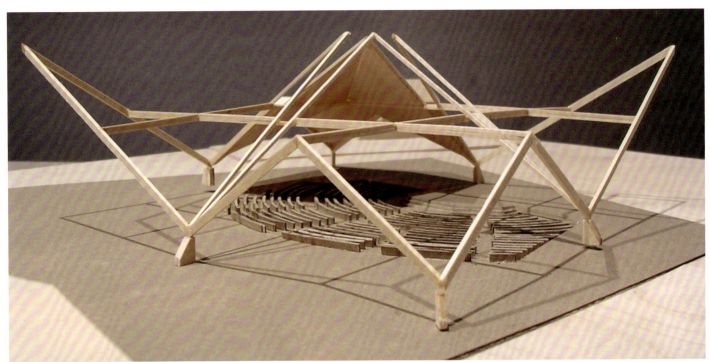

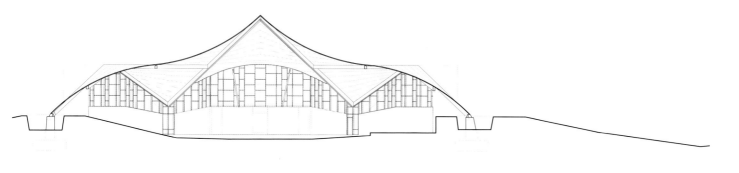

E/W Section

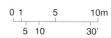

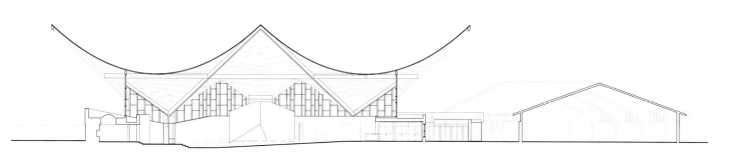

N/S Section

PENN CAFE AND COLLABORATORY
PHILADELPHIA, PA

The Penn Café and Collaboratory for Learning and Teaching is situated on two floors of the Van Pelt-Dietrich Library Center at the University of Pennsylvania.

The Collaboratory (1) and its services are intended to provide a stimulating intellectual center for improvement of traditional, problem-based, experimental learning, and original inquiry. It aims to improve students' abilities to understand and use new effective technologies to enhance their learning, communication, research, and the innovative skills of faculty and student teachers.

The Café (2) is intended to provide a respite for students where they can unwind from their studies in an indoor/outdoor environment.

The design intent of the Collaboratory is to bring together in, one shared workspace, previously disparate programs and staff in order to enhance academic success. The physical form of the Collaboratory is driven by the desire to enhance this pedagogical approach by allowing the users an opportunity to adapt, combine, experiment, plant, test, assess, and grow—encompassing, in microcosm, the essential functions of the University. The design utilizes a series of flexible meeting spaces (3) that allow for adaptive reconfiguration.

The design of the Café is derived from the creation of a minimal surface (4) that implies enclosure while maintaining visual connectivity to the spaces beyond. This form creates an envelope where students are separated from their studies without ever becoming detached. This ribbon-like form flows from one space to another, leading from intensive study to the indoor/outdoor café, all the while keeping them spatially tethered to the practice of learning.

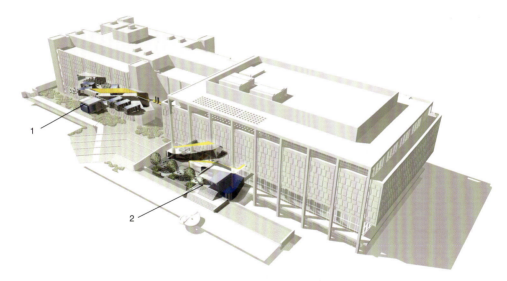

THE PIAZZA AT SCHMIDT'S COMMONS
PHILADELPHIA, PA

1071

THE PIAZZA AT SCHMIDT'S COMMONS
2003-2009

Experience is inextricably connected with place. Oftentimes experience is recorded in our memory according to the context in which it occurred. We recall the physical characteristics about the place where it happened, day-night, hot-cold, crowded-secluded etc. Experience is emotional and therefore much harder to describe.

The client for this urban, mixed-use project had been working with another architect to make a "Piazza" based on memories of a recent trip to Piazza Navona. He wanted to recreate that experience as part of the redevelopment of the former Schmidt's Brewery in Northern Liberties, a neighborhood just outside Center City Philadelphia. Together they had created a plan to wall off the piazza with decorated boxes applied with faux-Italianate ornamentation, an imitation of the client's memories of Rome. In reality, the planned architecture had little to do with what the place looked like: the experience he wanted to recreate was emotional. It was not the stucco façades, tiled roofs or wrought iron railings created his Rome experience. It was the social activity; a cup of espresso and a glass of wine amidst the bustle of market vendors and street performers.

The project faced strong opposition from the neighborhood zoning committee. At the committee's suggestion, Erdy McHenry Architecture was retained to re-imagine the development proposal. Considering the piazza as a social phenomenon rather than a physical one, the redesign of this project leverages the Public Square as more than the left over space between buildings to enable and provoke the emotive experience at the heart of any good urban space. The residential units are configured as bi-level loft units in a skip-stop configuration allowing each unit to maintain a connection to the piazza and views of the city while creating an activated façade both at the street and on the piazza. In addition, this strategic apartment layout reduced square footage and brought the apartments in dramatically under budget - allowing for the construction of an additional commercial building.

To promote a stronger connection with the neighborhood and the larger urban context, activity at street level is encouraged by a porous retail pattern. This creates passageways from the surrounding neighborhood to and through the piazza connecting to the transit stop and shopping areas. Cafes and restaurants entice pedestrians to linger. Programmed activities like fashion shows, flea markets, group yoga, and watch parties on the big screen embolden the visitor to become a participant and the prospect of community is strengthened.

The impact of this development echoes far beyond the immediate neighborhood context. The Piazza has become a sixth square to Thomas Holme's original plan for Philadelphia drafted at William Penn's direction upon founding this "City of Brotherly Love." In that sense, this community is connected well beyond a given floor or building but to the larger city of neighborhoods and to the lessons of urban planning tested and evolved over centuries.

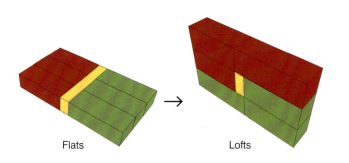

Flats → Lofts

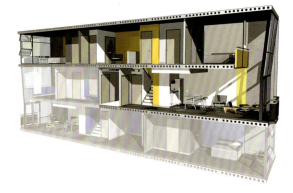

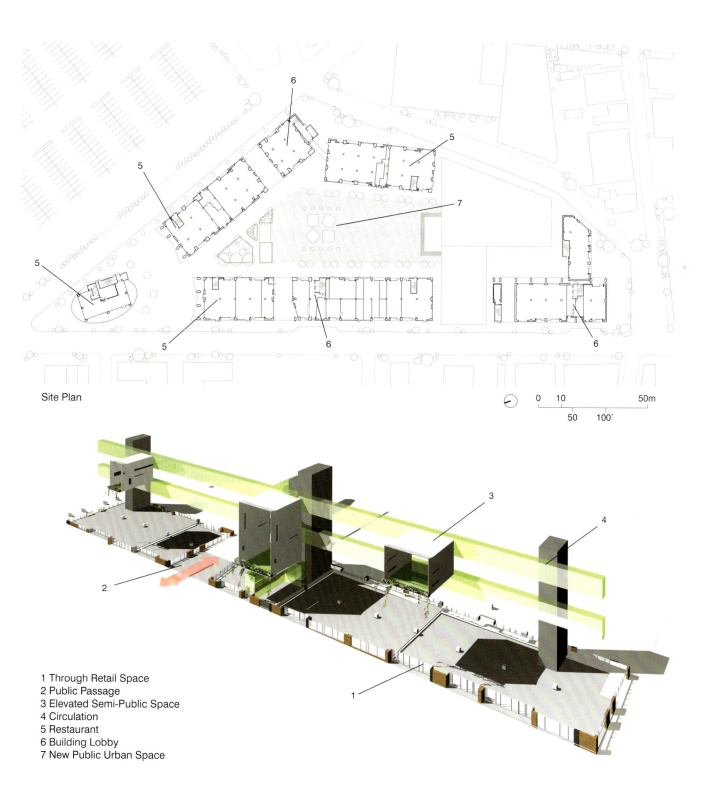

Site Plan

1 Through Retail Space
2 Public Passage
3 Elevated Semi-Public Space
4 Circulation
5 Restaurant
6 Building Lobby
7 New Public Urban Space

North Elevation

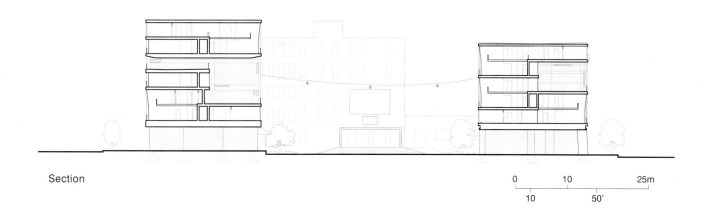

West Elevation

Section

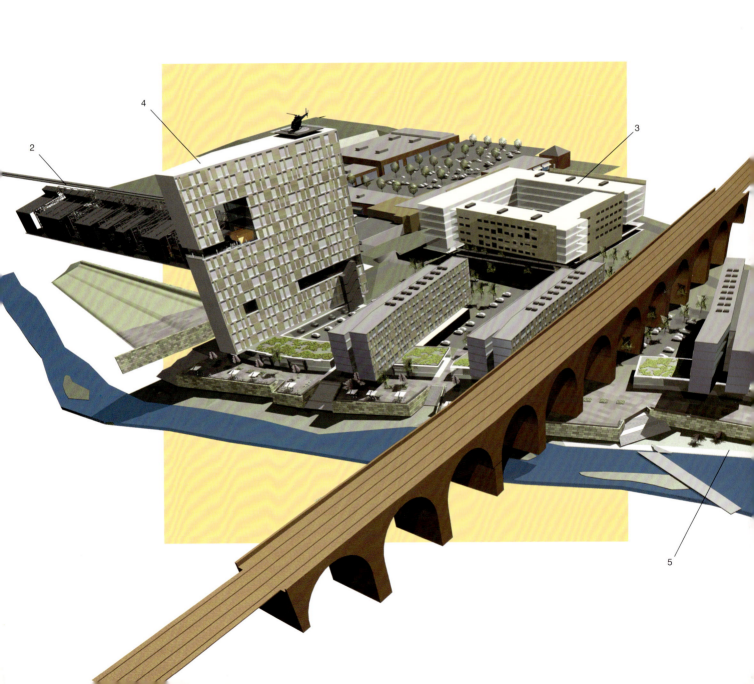

COATESVILLE REDEVELOPMENT
COATESVILLE, PA

In 1825, Lukens Steel Company rolled the plates for the Codorus, America's first iron-hulled vessel. It heralded the beginning of a long and successful relationship between Lukens and America's shipbuilding industry. Lukens played a significant role in the development of the transportation infrastructure of the United States, producing boilerplates for riverboat companies in New Orleans and Baldwin Locomotives for the Pennsylvania and many other Railroads, with national distribution enabled by the construction of the Philadelphia and Columbus Railroad in the 1830s.

During World War II, Lukens turned its attention to developments in heat-treated armor plate for naval vessels and military ground vehicles. The 1950s and 1960s saw continued expansion producing the hull plate for the first nuclear-powered submarine, the Nautilus; and steel for nuclear aircraft carriers, such as the Enterprise; oil tankers, such as the Manhattan; and skyscrapers, like the World Trade Center.

Coatesville's location along the Brandywine Creek (1) was central to its early development. The relative flatness of the valley allowed for agricultural development, and its proximity to the creek provided ample natural resources.

The city has been in decline since the end of the 1960s when several major changes to regional economics served to shift the economic prosperity of former decades away from Coatesville. Despite these conditions, Coatesville is poised for transformation. The redevelopment project aims to recall the vitality of the once booming steel town. The master plan calls for large-scale construction, which will create new jobs for the area and a sense of excitement that only comes with this type of economic resurgence.

A highlight of the new master plan is the redevelopment of an existing mill building (2). The former mill will be stabilized and refurbished in selected areas while peeling off 75% of the enclosure to allow for the insertion of a commercial shopping center (3) with apartments above. Immediately north of the Lincoln Highway is a high-rise, mixed use building (4). Situated in-line with the Lincoln Highway as it runs through the Central Business District, it will be a marker of the new development and will symbolize the city's transition from a steel town to a new urban destination.

The northern end of the site features four mid-rise, mixed use buildings oriented towards the new river-walk (5), a pedestrian promenade, which is lined with retail and restaurant spaces. The area will be activated both day and night, as there is an appropriate mix of commercial and residential above. The re-development is continued north of the railway to spread activity along the wide banks of the Brandywine Creek.

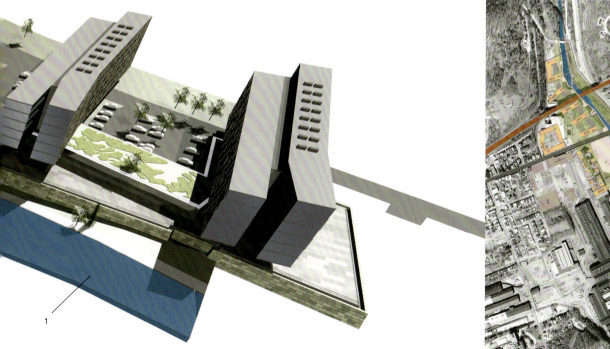

1077
AVENUE NORTH
PHILADELPHIA, PA

AVENUE NORTH
2004-2007

Town-gown issues are not new. Host communities to colleges and universities understandably struggle to find a balance between the potential economic benefits offered by the institution's investments and a desire for the community to maintain a unique identity. Meanwhile, there is an expectation that both the institution and the community will have an equal voice in shared interests. Successful relationships grow from repeated interaction rooted in cooperation and trust. In contrast, a pattern of unilateral action on the part of the institution threatens the community's sense of independence and undermines any opportunity for cooperation to leverage mutual interest. Balancing each party's need for individual mission and aspiration with the essential recognition of a mutually beneficial interdependence is where successful projects can take root.

A series of failed attempts to redevelop this vacant site on the border between Temple University and the adjacent North Philadelphia neighborhood evidenced a deep-seated legacy of mistrust. Bridging that divide necessitated a mixed use development strategy that would maximize the allowable FAR for the developer while finding the right mix of uses that balanced the needs of the University with the expectations of their host community.

After several breakfast meetings with several neighborhood groups, two things became clear: the community was not opposed to the presence of the University, after all it grew out of the neighborhood in the original founding by Russell Conwell. What seemed to frustrate them was the fact that the University had turned its back on the neighborhood, seeing it as an inventory of potentially available real estate to fuel its seemingly insatiable growth. Secondly, and partly as a result of the first point, the neighborhood was grossly under-served in terms of community services and quality retail options, not the least of which was the fact that they had lost their only neighborhood movie theater that fell into disrepair and was torn down just blocks from this location—a simple but fundamental obstacle to finding common ground.

In the end, the key to making this program of 1,200 beds of student housing and 90,000 SF of retail work in this complex context was rooted in a residential lease provision prohibiting students from having a car on campus. This greatly reduced the required parking, which enabled a site strategy based on affinity of use rather than territorial delineation. Retail uses were positioned on the campus side of the site fronting Broad Street, including a second-floor multiplex movie theater, while the student housing was situated on the neighborhood side of the site. The object and intent of this approach was to blur the dividing line between campus and neighborhood in favor of uniting the communities by shared retail and amenities that served the needs of both. This approach also allowed us to preserve a row of existing buildings that helped to stitch old and new in the fabric of the neighborhood and did the same for the partnership between town and gown.

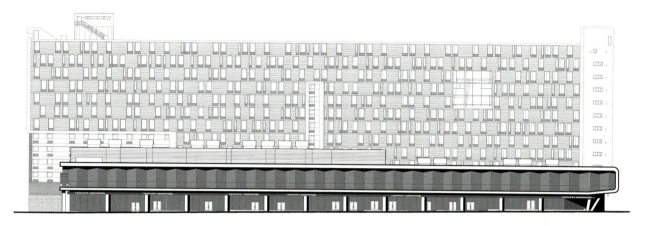

East Elevation

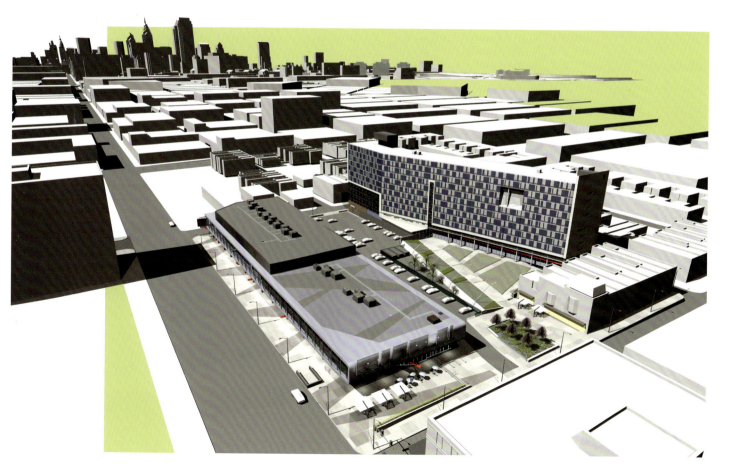

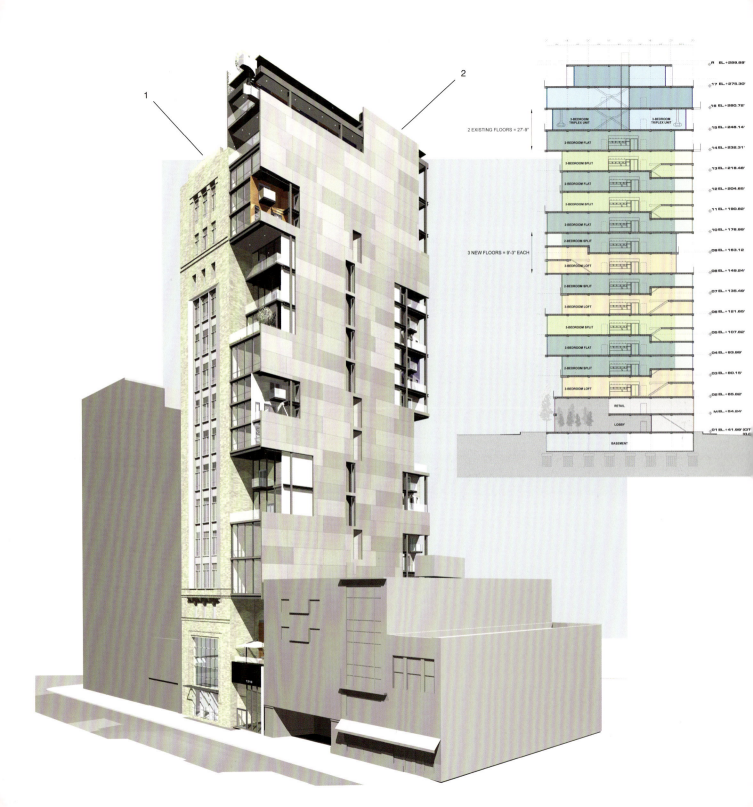

1093 CUNNINGHAM PIANO BUILDING
PHILADELPHIA, PA

Host|Parasite Mutualism:
A Guide to a Successful Preservation Strategy

Nature can teach us about systems, materials, processes, structures and legible expressions of function. By delving more deeply into how nature solves problems, we can derive new solutions for our built environments and, more particularly, how we reconcile preservation responsibilities in the way that our built environment evolves over time and technologies.

All artifacts reflect the technologies and customs of their time. The evolution of our built environment and the artifacts that survive as worthy of "preservation" become part of the fabric woven out of those evolutionary artifacts. As we build today, we must be respectful of those resources without being replicative or we stunt the logical evolution of who we are as reflected in the remnants that we will leave behind. The cultural aspects that make a place unique or contribute to its character and charm evolved in a context. The roots and evolution of that context—physical, chronological, intellectual and archeological—must be preserved and promoted if the culture is to continue to evolve.

Preservation, far from being a hindrance to economic growth, can be a fundamental enabler to economic development. While we would all like to believe that preservation would be self-motivated and self-sustaining, the reality is that preservation will always require external pressure and incentives to make it a beneficial approach rather than the best alternative among an otherwise less desirable set of options.

Economic strategies and real estate development success rely heavily on leverage – using someone else's money, negotiating entitlements or enabling legislation that yield a project specific benefit by transferring risk or deferring cost to someone else. In this light, existing historic buildings or existing context – which may be a single historical structure or an entire neighborhood that contributes to the identification of "place" – are oftentimes viewed as obstacles to redevelopment. The goal of the designer is to find and illuminate the benefit of preserving these structures that so strongly define place and historical character.

The Cunningham Piano Building (1), completed in 1924, exists at mid-block with 4,000 SF floor plates with access to light and air only at its frontage on Chestnut Street and the rear alley on Drury Street. Rendered obsolete as an office building by modern standards, the building would face an uncertain future. Its best chance of preservation was rooted in a repurposing leveraged by a host-parasite strategy that allowed the underlying asset to be accessed in a way that would not otherwise be possible.

The new construction utilizes surplus dead-load capacity in the existing building's structure and in return, provides lateral bracing to the existing building that would not otherwise be able to satisfy more stringent seismic code requirements for high-rise buildings. Additionally the new construction utilizes the existing stairs and elevators for vertical transportation and the historic floor-to-floor heights to create interstitial levels in the new construction yielding a net-to-gross ratio approaching 130 percent.

The proposed intervention is a seventeen-story condominium tower (2) that slides into place beside The Cunningham Building. The primary gesture is that of a paired slab that is sliced and peeled back to reveal the form of the original building and the stunning views of its dense Center City environment.

It is rather provocative to consider how incorporating a historic structure into a project becomes a primary financial leverage to create a Return on Investment beyond anything that could be generated from a vacant lot.

Typical Floor Plan

1097
THE RADIAN
PHILADELPHIA, PA

THE RADIAN
2006-2011

This mid-block development adjacent to the campus of the University of Pennsylvania came to us rather unexpectedly. Around the same time that we were completing our first student housing project at Avenue North, the University of Pennsylvania issued a request for proposal to developers seeking a public-private partnership. The program was to develop 500 beds of student housing, along with supporting retail on a university-owned parcel on the edge of campus with frontage on Walnut Street and Sansom Street. We had tried to get on one of the development teams with a local developer but were not successful.

A few months had passed when we received a phone call from the developer who had been selected by Penn to execute the project. They were struggling with the level of experience on the part of their design team with urban mixed-use. The question posed by the developer on that call was whether we would be willing to join their team as "architect-of-record" to work with their current architect in their role as "design architect". We recognized this moment for what it was. Taking on the role of architect-of-record would have set our practice on an unintended trajectory at odds with everything we held sacred when we took the risk in leaving a big firm to set out on our own. We declined. There was a long pause on the phone. The silence was broken when the developer asked us to take over the project and assemble our own team. Patience paid off.

The mid-block condition was a significant challenge for a project of this magnitude. We made the challenge more difficult when we opted to keep a row of existing houses that fronted on Sansom Street. The context operated at a variety of scales, with the grand proportions of a significant campus green across Walnut Street acting in contrast to the intimate character of Sansom. The low-rise context of retail along Walnut required a sensitive approach to placement and massing of the inevitable residential tower necessary to accommodate the program. Sansom Street presented a more significant challenge if the desire to create a walkable street with sidewalk dining, similar to the 3400 block, was to be achieved.

Reconciling these disparate influences, the massing strategy places a folded tower on a plinth to optimize available view corridors and to reduce the apparent mass to the pedestrian and adjacent streetscape. The relationship between tower and plinth is articulated by raising the tower on pilotis, introducing skyplane vistas at the intersection of the two primary masses. The bend of the tower defines a public terrace and green roof activated by a restaurant and beer garden that occupy the soft story between the residential upper stories and ground floor retail.

Amenity spaces on the upper floors are revealed by significant articulations in the mass of the tower, while a distributed pattern of window openings in the pressure-balanced rainscreen façade telegraphs the integrated unit mix and diverse social structure of the residential program.

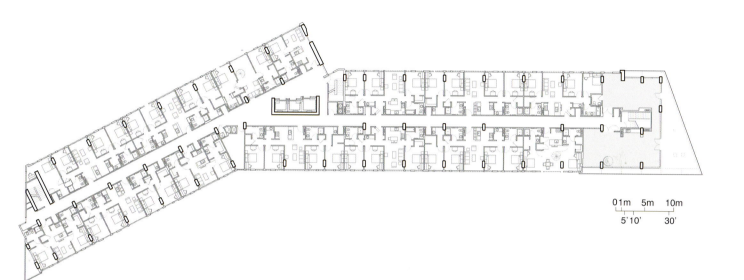

Level 09 Floor Plan

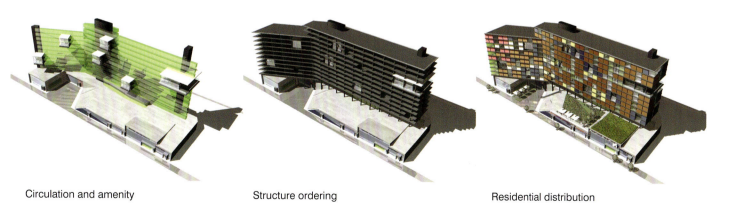

Circulation and amenity   Structure ordering   Residential distribution

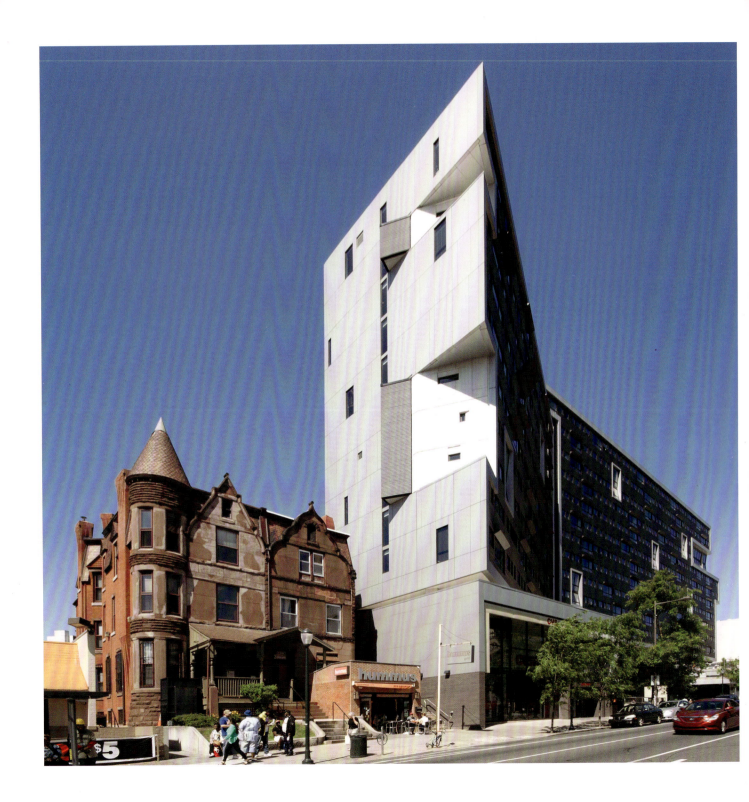

1 Roof Terrace
2 Grand Stair
3 Residential
4 Double Height Living Space
5 Street Level Retail Space

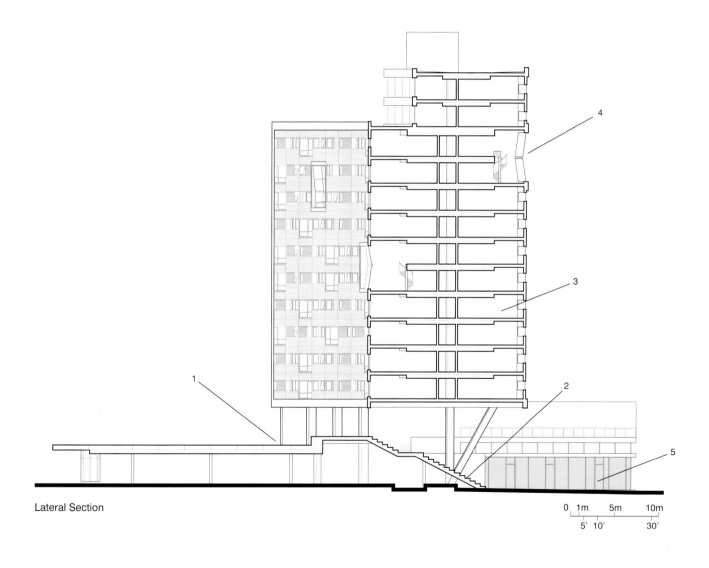

Lateral Section

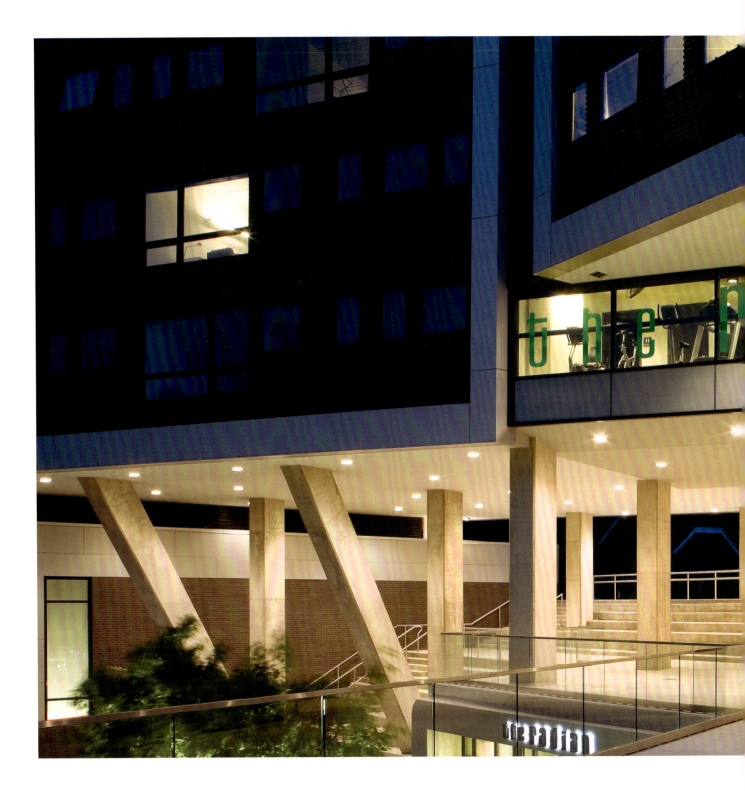

1098
INDEPENDENCE MALL CAFE
PHILADELPHIA, PA

INDEPENDENCE MALL CAFE
2006-2008

As part of a broader urban renewal program in Philadelphia's oldest commercial district, the creation of Independence Mall State Park was realized between 1950 and 1967. Roy F. Larson's initial Beaux Arts plan for the mall was given a more Modernist style by Edmund Bacon, director of the Philadelphia City Planning Commission, with the intention that the land would eventually be turned over to the National Park Service as part of the larger Independence National Historical Park.

The mall has seen several periods of renovation since its completion in 1967, including the construction of a controversial pavilion to house the Liberty Bell designed by Romaldo Giurgola which opened on January 1, 1976 as part of the bicentennial celebration in Philadelphia. The bell remained there until 2003 when the pavilion was removed and the bell relocated to its new home at 6th and Arch Streets. Most recently, the Olin Master Plan proposed the removal of all previous structures, except the Free Quaker Meetinghouse. It situated all of the proposed buildings along 6th Street at the western edge of the park with smaller pocket parks along 5th Street to the east. The smaller parks along the eastern edge, some of which were raised above the central lawn, would provide more intimate gathering and sitting areas with extensive trees and other landscaping. The plan imagined that these informal areas would be supported by a series of vendor kiosks offering refreshments to visitors similar to Bryant Park in New York.

Erdy McHenry Architecture was retained to design and oversee the construction of these kiosks coincident with the larger renovation of the mall. At the outset of this project the executive director of Independence Visitor Center Corporation charged the design team with investigating a solution suitable for the sacred ground of Independence Mall that would not require a subsidized operation. In order to reconcile the intent of the master plan with the economic constraints imposed by the Visitor Center, the Erdy McHenry design introduced three fundamental strategies: instead of multiple kiosks, a single pavilion was proposed to streamline operational overhead; the pavilion was perched atop the existing perimeter retaining wall along 5th Street to make itself known to local and out-of-town patrons alike rather than relying on the occasional tourist to happen upon it; lastly, the pavilion which would have no heat or air conditioning was designed as a three-season structure that would extend its operating season employing passive strategies for heating and cooling. The new cafe consciously avoids superficial or cosmetic attempts at compatibility in form or material with the historically significant buildings that give context to the mall. Rather, the cafe abandons symbolic representation by confirming the continuity of the future and present with the past by a fresh, modern reinterpretation. Simple materials are detailed minimally and quietly. The warmth of the weathering steel cladding is compatible with the traditional red brick so prevalent in Old City. Wood as a simple wrapper becomes floor, wall and ceiling, warmly defining the public areas. Glass walls fold away allowing flexibility and the conveyance of openness.

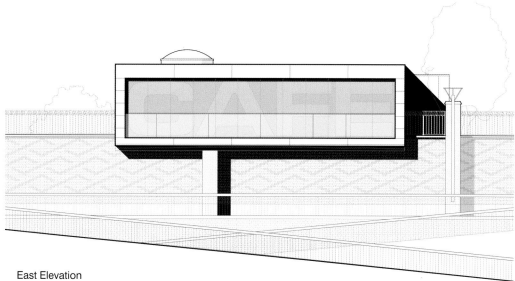

East Elevation

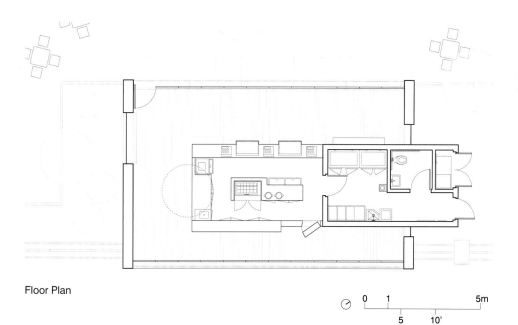

Floor Plan

1104
3 CRESCENT DRIVE
PHILADELPHIA, PA

3 CRESCENT DRIVE
2007-2010

The Philadelphia Naval Shipyard, commissioned by Congress in 1799, is situated on League Island at the confluence of the Schuylkill and Delaware Rivers. The Shipyard continued to operate as a naval base until 1996, employing more than 40,000 people during its peak production period in World War II. During that time, 53 warships were constructed, and an additional 1,218 were repaired. The Base Realignment and Closure Commission (BRAC) made the decision to cease operations in 1991 and after a lengthy court challenge and political maneuvering, the Philadelphia Naval Shipyard closed on September 26, 1996. Since its closure a combination of publicly funded infrastructure improvements and significant private investment has transformed a 1,200-acre portion of the former Navy facility into the most successful commercial redevelopment of a former military facility anywhere in the country. Three Crescent Drive is a four-story 100,000 SF speculative office building anchoring the corner of Crescent Drive and Rouse Boulevard, becoming the first building in the overall master plan to occupy this main axis of the Navy Yard. The building shares frontage on Crescent Drive with two other building forming a triptych that defined Crescent Park at the main entrance to the Navy Yard. The prominent location and visibility from Interstate 95. The building is sited in an urban condition fronting on the two main streets, Crescent and Rouse. The opposite sides of the building fronts on surface parking at a ratio similar to suburban sites. This planning configuration and convenient access to center City Philadelphia has proven to be very desirable to corporate tenants looking for that sweet spot between the city and the suburbs.

The flood plain condition throughout most of the Navy Yard necessitates a raised plinth that gives the buildings a unique character at the pedestrian scale reminiscent of a classical urban condition. Along Crescent Drive, the curving glass façade is lifted up and the ground floor pushed back to reflect the importance of the intersection of Rouse Boulevard, the main arterial access to the masterplan. Passersby are invited up to the covered plinth walkway by a monumental stair which passes between sloping planting beds. An angled bay window projects from the Crescent Drive façade on the second and third floors, offering tenants a direct view north to the city skyline. A terrace above on the fourth floor, as well as projecting balconies on the lower floors, afford views of the battleships docked in the basin beyond, while recalling the form and industrial nature of naval design. The exterior of the building is clad in a custom designed system of shingled fiber cement panels in homage to the lapped steel cladding of the battleships and frigates moored in the adjacent boat basin. The alternating panels give the building an ever-changing skin, depending on the time of day and amount of sunlight. Configured around an internal atrium, the clerestory glazing washes down an undulating bamboo panel wall to diffuse the direct sunlight and to allow the color of the light to be warmed by the natural wood before filtering into offices and down to the lobby below. The wall is hidden from the exterior, only revealing itself upon entering the building.

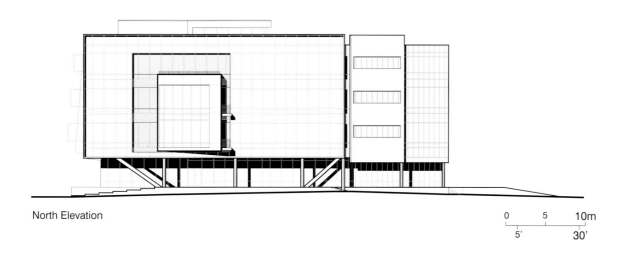

North Elevation

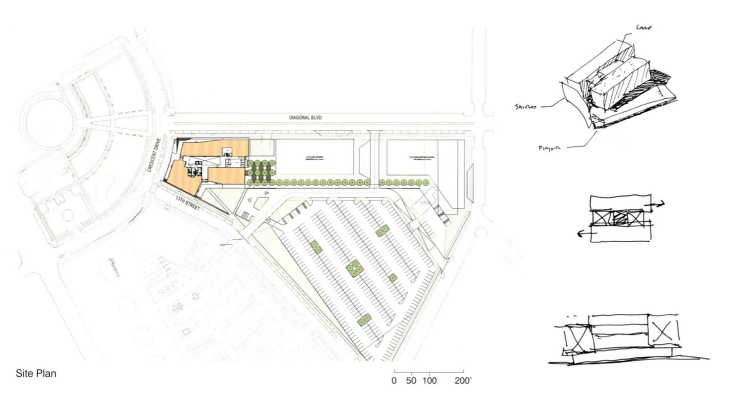

Site Plan

1107

MILLENNIUM HALL
PHILADELPHIA, PA

1137   Courtyard Marriott - Ensemble Hotel Partners - Navy Yard

1138   Brandywine Realty Trust

1139   LPT Great Valley Design Competition

1140   The 10,000 Friends of Pennsylvania Commonwealth Awards: Diamond Award for a Private Project: The Piazza at Schmidt's / Washington University in St. Louis

1141   Albany Medical Center (MDC)

1142   Evo Cira Green South - Chestnut Tower
- Temple University Library
- Peak Campus Development - Universecit Chicago / Stony Island Site Student Housing
- Upenn Summer Studio
- Open House
- In Articulation Lecture at Temple

1143   AIA Philadelphia Merit Award - Built Category: 330 Cooper Street
- Casualty lecture and exhibition at Syracuse University

1144   UPC Stony Island Student Housing

1145   Cira Skygreen - Cira South Garage Green Roof
- Penn Library Innovative Classroom
- UCD Social Seating

1146   Liberty Property Trust - Subaru North American Headquarters
- Brandywine Queen Lane Site

1147   Architectural Record "The Cows Come Home" (Cover Story)
- Campus Crest Communities

1148   Uncommon IIVA - Campus Acquisitions Charlottesville

1149   Campus Acquisitions Morgantown WV
- Virginia Tech Keyland Facilities

1150   PENN Medicine - PCAM South Tower

1151   AIA Central NY Citation for Design Residential: Multi-Family Project - Syracuse Law College Housing
- AIA Philadelphia Gold Medal - Built Category: Cornell University Teaching Dairy Barn
- AIA Philadelphia Merit Award - Built Category: Vertical Screen Corporate Headquarters
- AIA Philadelphia Honor Award - Unbuilt Category: Cira Sky Green
- AIA New York State Design Awards - Citation for Design: Cornell University Teaching Dairy Barn
- 6 Grays Ferry Parkway - LPT 5 Country View Repositioning

1152   LRF Development Jersey City

1153   CAI Columbus OHI

1154   COPT + SSG Woodlands I
- Penn State - Digester Dairy Barn
- Penn State - Brandywine Housing
- Penn State - Abington Housing

1155   Vue32 - RPG 3201 Race Mixed Use
- Open House
- Penn State - East Halls Renovation

1156   Ballerman I Allaire Building E

1157   Piazza Mgmt Co. - Concept Study - BPG 700 N Delaware
- Interpark LLC - LOVE Park Renovation
- Design Philadelphia Open House
- NOMA Conference
- AIA Pennsylvania Architectural Excellence Honor Award: Cornell University Teaching Dairy Barn
- AIA Philadelphia Merit Award - Built Category: Courtyard Philadelphia South
- Brandywine Realty - 3020 Market Street
- AIA Panel - Digital Modeling

1158   GSA Green Federal Building

1159   Holly Pointe Commons - USL Rowan Student Housing

1160   Ensemble PNY Extended Stay
- PNY Marriott Expansion (ICI-DB)

1161   Global Innovation Center - LPT PNY Axalta

1162   COPT Northridge
- Design Philadelphia Open House

1163   SLC 3750 Lancaster Ave
- University of Pennsylvania - Van Pelt Reading Room
- AIA Philadelphia Honor Award - Built Category: EVO and Sky Green at Cira Centre South
- AIA Philadelphia Silver Medal - Unbuilt Category: PennDesign Meyerson Hall Transformation
- DVGBC Ground Breaker Award - Cira Green
- NCSEA 2015 - Structural Engineering Award - Outstanding Project over $100 million - Evo and Cira Green at Cira Centre South
- The 10,000 Friends of Pennsylvania Commonwealth Award - Residential Project: Evo and Cira Green at Cira Centre South
- American Bible Society - Museum of the American Bible

1164   OSU CFAES Study/Master Plan (Finley Farm, Don Scott Field, Waterman Lab, Wooster?)

1165   Lumpkin's Jail Interpretive Center-City of Richmond

*1166   USL Syracuse East Genesee (505 Walnut)
- Lumpkin's Jail-City of Richmond

1167   Nodsul Dream Island (Competition)

1168   Rowan SOM Master Plan

1169   Valeo LIV (Miami & Birmingham)
- AIA Convention Open House
- Nodsul Dream Island Competition

MILLENNIUM HALL
2007-2011

This project, perhaps more than any other, illustrates the delicate interrelationships between program, budget, and schedule that drives all projects. Often aspiration and intent are at odds with allocated resources or constrained by conventional thinking. In the case of Millennium Hall, the program anticipated 500 beds for Drexel University students in traditional suites on a site occupied by three tennis courts. The solicitation contemplated an architecturally "significant" building but allocated a budget that was substantially less than the average per-bed cost in the market at the time and the urgent demand for on-campus housing necessitated a schedule that was justifiably aggressive.

Resolution of these incongruities led to a shared path of discovery between us and the University. A series of focus groups with students and staff led to residential strategy founded on a social and intellectual infrastructure that aligns residents based on extracurricular interest. Each residential floor is organized as a suite with of double-occupancy bedrooms sharing the necessary residential services distributed about the core area. The intimacy of this approach necessitated a smaller floor plate more appropriate to the confined site. The accumulated program adjustment resulted in an overall gross square footage one-third smaller than that which would have been required by the traditional suite style design.

Working with Arup's Advanced Geometry Unit, we developed a structural approach that established a ring of columns around the core that served as a cage from which the upper floors were cantilevered. We rotated the cage ten inches per floor, introducing a twist in the building, to reorient the rooftop lounge back to dramatic views of the Center City skyline while giving the tower a remarkable presence on the University City skyline. The cage and cantilever structural approach also enabled us to substantially reduce the footprint at grade and thereby limit the area of disturbance and avoid a more lengthy review and approval process. This in turn accelerated the building permit and pulled forward the occupancy date one full year.

Once construction of the building was started, we submitted a separate package for master plan improvements associated with the adjacent green space which included the site improvements associated with the new residential tower.

Programmed and designed with a desire to understand and support the social structure of student life, Millennium Hall has become the honors dorm for the University and one of the most sought after housing options on campus.

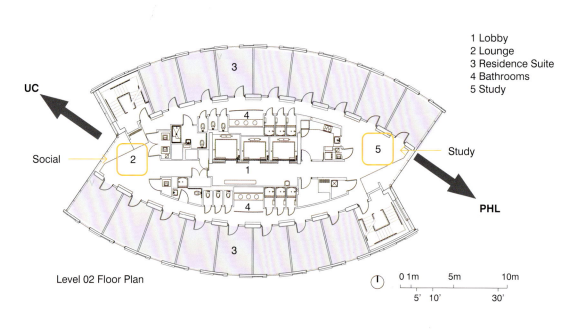

UC ← Social — 2

5 — Study → PHL

1 Lobby
2 Lounge
3 Residence Suite
4 Bathrooms
5 Study

Level 02 Floor Plan

0 1m   5m   10m
5' 10'   30'

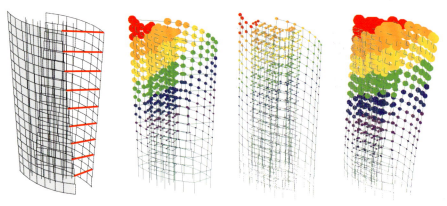

Structural Analysis Diagrams
ARUP Advanced Geometry Unit

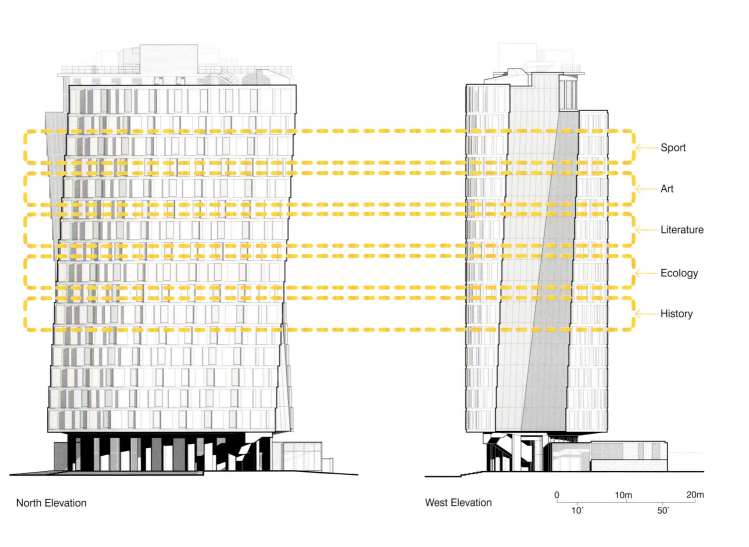

1116
VERTICAL SCREEN
WARMINSTER, PA

VERTICAL SCREEN
2008-2011

Employee training and retention costs are becoming increasingly important in today's employment market, particularly with an increasing proportion of job-hopping millennials in the workforce. Vertical Screen understood the need to appeal to this segment of the workforce and the workplace environment and culture is high on their list of priorities. At the same time, contemplating a consolidation of multiple leased facilities into one headquarters site weighed heavily on the mid of its CEO. He recognized that constructing a new headquarters facility would constitute the most significant impact on the environment that he would make in his lifetime. He opted to make choices that would make that impact a positive outcome and charged the design team accordingly. Vertical Screen Corporate Headquarters was constructed on a former brownfield site that once served as the Naval Air Warfare Center which included the training facility for America's Mercury, Gemini, and Apollo space programs. Vertical Screen's new facility sits on a nine-acre parcel that includes what was once the runway of this former Navy facility. The 49,600 SF commercial office building, located in Warminster, Pennsylvania, is designed to house up to 450 employees. With sufficient site area to construct additional square footage as part of a phased expansion when that became necessary.

The design embraces the site's historic past by taking on the iconic form of an aircraft hangar—a large singular volume supported by 11 barrel-shaped glulam beams with a 144-foot clear span that provides an open office flooded with natural daylight. Interior green roofs and a vegetated wall contribute to improved indoor air quality. The high-bay workspace is located in the 'garden zone', an open area where employees can enjoy views of the natural meadow. The building's east and west façades are comprised entirely of low-E glazing, enhancing opportunities for daylight and views to the exterior and providing building users with a visual connection to the adjacent environment. 900 roof-mounted Solyndra photovoltaic panels generate 164 kilowatts of power and provide 20% of the building's energy requirements. A rainwater harvesting system collects rainwater from the roof and stores it in a 50,000 gallon storage tank used to flush low-flow toilet fixtures and to irrigate interior plants and site landscaping. Light control, daylight-harvesting zones and motion sensors control all interior office lighting. Individual desk task lights use motion sensors to reduce overall electrical usage by 60% compared to a typical office building. FSC-certified wood products were used in the building along with bamboo casework and doors, recycled glass counter tops, and recycled tire carpeting.

Upon its completion this project received LEED Platinum Certification with a score of 58 points, making it the greenest building in the Commonwealth of Pennsylvania, tied for the seventh-highest LEED score in the United States, and ninth highest in the world. The building also functions as an educational facility, available for tours to share information about environmental technologies with students or other businesses interested in creating sustainable work environments.

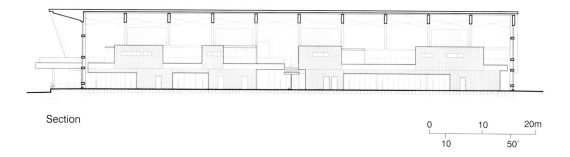

Section

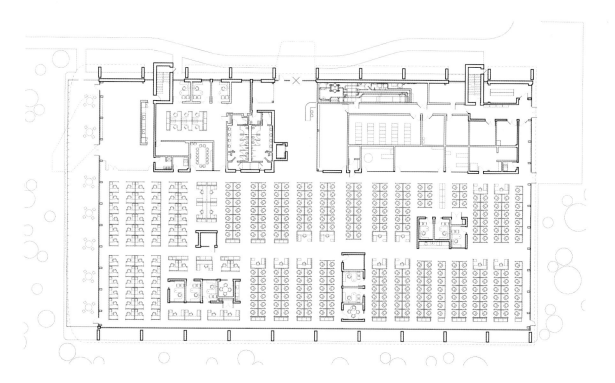

Ground Floor Plan

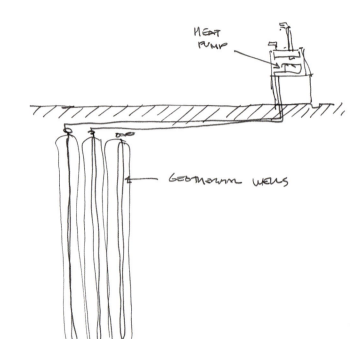

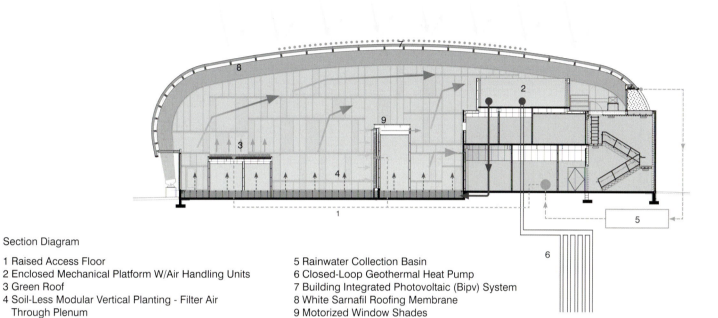

Section Diagram

1 Raised Access Floor
2 Enclosed Mechanical Platform W/Air Handling Units
3 Green Roof
4 Soil-Less Modular Vertical Planting - Filter Air Through Plenum
5 Rainwater Collection Basin
6 Closed-Loop Geothermal Heat Pump
7 Building Integrated Photovoltaic (Bipv) System
8 White Sarnafil Roofing Membrane
9 Motorized Window Shades

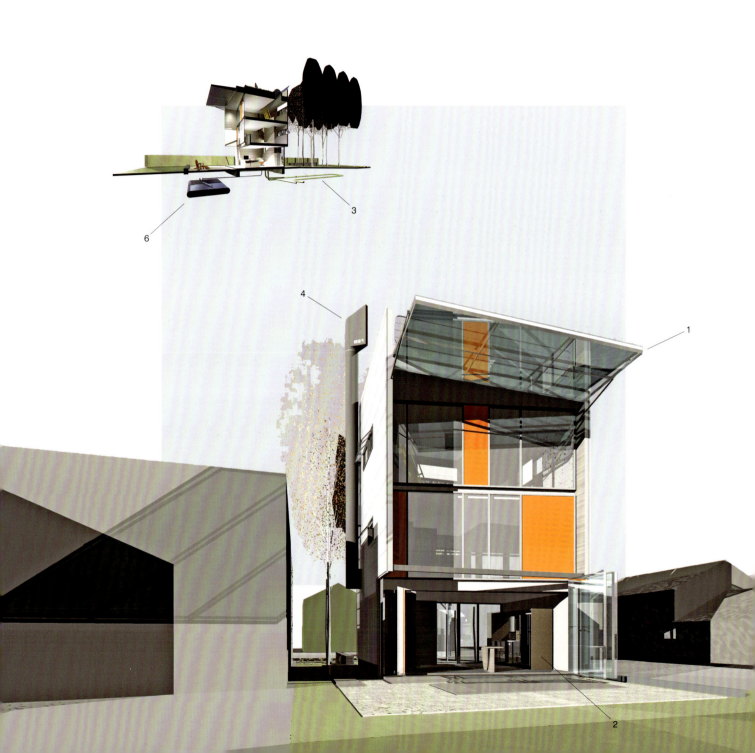

1118

LUMEN-AIR HOUSE
SYRACUSE, NY

The Lumen-Air House was designed in collaboration with Professor Tim Stenson for Upstate, an interdisciplinary center for design, research and real estate founded at the School of Architecture at Syracuse University.

Upstate was seeking a sustainable and economical house that would breathe life back into Syracuse's Near Westside neighborhood. Crucial to Upstate's mission was the practicality, affordability, and adaptability of the house. Per Upstate's market research, the project would need to be a 1,100—1,500 square foot home containing four bedrooms that could be built for under $150,000, including fees and site work. The final product would need to represent an example of cutting-edge, sustainable practices, but shouldn't leave the user feeling as though they were living in an architectural experiment.

The joys of Syracuse weather bring about the challenges of designing high performance, low energy housing in the surrounding area. In August, it is 82 degrees with a pleasant westerly breeze, but in February it's 15 degrees with a rather unpleasant northwest wind. The challenge is not simply to design a house, but to design two houses in one—a multi-mode environmental device.

The Lumen-Air House is a machine for living. In the warmer months the house opens via a large glass hangar door (1), to filtering sunlight and allowing the free flow of fresh air. For the cold gray winter it buttons up. The interior living spaces (2) are protected, insulated, by thermal buffer zones on the north and south faces. Though closed down, the interior of the house glows with diffused daylight through the multiple layers of greenhouse enclosure. In the warmer seasons, the open-closed aspect of the house adjusts to the changing weather and is augmented by a series of earth tubes (3) which take advantage of the consistent ground temperatures. A ventilation stack draws fresh air into the building through the negative pressure created by its weather vein type snoot (4). The result is a house that engages directly and intimately with the weather and environment throughout the entire year.

The extensive vegetable planter located on the roof (5) benefits from rainwater harvesting and a grey water recycling system (6). The garden is capable of producing enough calories in the summer months to support a family of 5 and still have left over produce for friends, family, and surrounding neighbors.

The Lumen-Air House does not intend to camouflage into its surroundings. To the contrary, the house posits a conspicuous and yet critical complement to the character of the Near Westside neighborhood. The house is optimistic, outwardly asserting that architecture can efficiently respond to climate and provide shelter, comfort and environmental benefit.

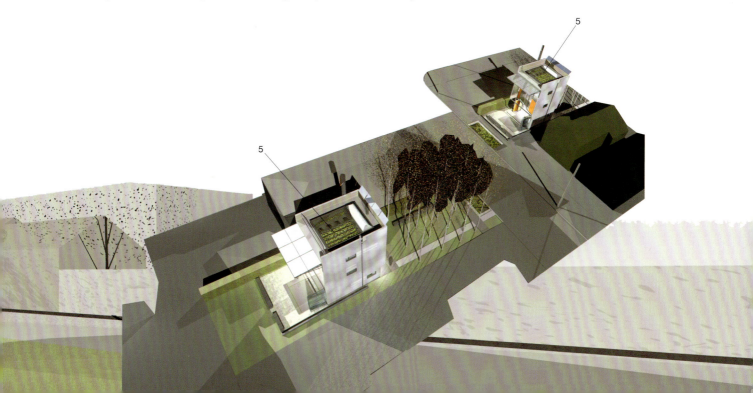

1113 Philadelphia Water Department, Office of Watersheds, Best Stormwater Management Practices: The Radian
GBCA Construction Excellence Award: Best Design Built Project – Drexel University Residence Hall
1114 CRRC Jumping Brook
Bollerman Parkway Falls
1115 Parkway Corp. 23rd & Market
1116 Vertical Screen - Warminster
Michaels Development - Cooper Housing
1117 Architectural Record "Urban Multifamily Housing: Fringe Benefits" featuring One Brewerytown Square
Architectural Record "NoLi Housing"
Philadelphia Inquirer "Changing Skyline – Adding Coffee to the Culture (Independence Mall Café)"
1118 Lumen-Air House - Syracuse - From The Ground Up
Open House
1119 Drexel Dining Terrace
AIA National Housing Award: NoLi Housing
AIA Philadelphia Honor Award: Built Category: Independence Mall Café
AIA Montgomery Alabama Chapter Honorable Mention: Southern Poverty Law Center
DBIA Pennsylvania Tri-State Region Design-Build Project Award: Drexel University Race Street Residence Hall
GBCA Construction Excellence Award: Best Design Built Project – Drexel University Residence Hall
1120 Cornell Teaching Dairy Barn
1121 Syracuse Intermodal Trans. Center
1122 Goldman Cafe District Visioning
Lights of Liberty
1123 Metal Architecture Magazine "Divine Dwelling"
Synterra Pnrs Broad & Spring Garden
1124 330 Cooper Street - MDC - CCIA Rutgers Housing Camden
1125 Campus Living Villages
1126 SU Law College Housing (Campus West)
Enterprise Center
Fertile Ground Exhibition
1127 Mariana Bracetti Academy
The New York Times "From Abandoned Brewery to Piazza, Family-Style" by Terri Pristin
AIA Philadelphia Honor Award – Unbuilt Category: Lumen-Air House
AIA Philadelphia Merit Award – Built Category: The Piazza at Schmidt's
AIA Philadelphia Merit Award – Built Category: The Radian
Metal Construction Association President's Award: Roofing – St. Aloysius of Gonzaga Church
Metal Architecture Magazine, Metal Roofing Award, St. Aloysius Church, Jackson, NJ
McGraw Hill Mid-Atlantic Construction Award of Merit Higher Education/Research: Drexel University Millennium Hall, Philadelphia
McGraw Hill New York Construction's Best of 2009 Project of the Year Worship: The Church of St. Aloysius-Jackson, N.J.
McGraw Hill New York Construction's Best of 2009 judges' Award: Best Architectural Design – The Church of St. Aloysius-Jackson, N.J.
GBCA Construction Excellence Award: Best Design Built Project: Best Commercial Project Over $15 Million – The Radian
Best Overall Design Build Project, PA Region – Drexel University Race Street Residence Hall
Philadelphia Inquirer "City's Green Groundbreakers" (Firm Profile) by Inga Saffron
1128 University of the Arts
1129 PPMC M,O,B./Surgery Center
Ministry & Liturgy "St. Aloysius, A Tent for a Pilgrim People" by G. Scott Shaffer
1130 Goldman - Newark City
Open House
1131 Railroad Museum of PA (DGS)
1132 East Baltimore Community School
1133 PennDesign Renovation (Stuart Weitzman School of Design)
AIA Pennsylvania Architectural Excellence in Design Citation of Merit Award: The Radian
GBCA Construction Excellence Award: Best Industrial/Institutional Project Under $15 Million – Drexel University Northside Dining Terrace
GBCA Construction Excellence Award: Best Industrial/Institutional Project Under $15 Million – Drexel University Millennium Hall
Eastern Pennsylvania & Delaware Chapter American Concrete Institute Grand Prize Award for Cast in Place: Millennium Hall Student Residence at Drexel University
1134 Drexel Learning Terrace (ICI)
Delaware Valley Regional Planning Commission – Regional Land Use Program of the Year: The Piazza at Schmidt's Common
1135 Realen Convention Center Parking Facility (1324-1338 Arch)
Philadelphia Inquirer "Changing Skyline: Vertical Screen building offers bright ideas for cubicle slaves" May 20, 2011 Inga Saffron
Bucks County Courier Times "New Vertical Screen headquarters puts green on display" June 2011 - Crissa Shoemaker DeBreeSt
Beth Sholom Congregation
1136 LPT Commerce Center Bldg 3
1137 Courtyard Marriott - Ensemble Hotel Partners - Navy Yard
1138 Brandywine Realty Trust
1139 LPT Great Valley Design Competition
The 10,000 Friends of Pennsylvania Commonwealth Awards: Bernard Award for Design Project – The Piazza at Schmidt's
1140 Washington University in St. Louis
1141 Albany Medical Center (MDC)
Evo Cira Centre South - Chestnut Tower
1142 Temple University Library
Peak Campus Development – University of Chicago / Stony Island Site/Student Housing
Upenn Summer Studio
Open House
In Articulation : lecture at Temple
1143 AIA Philadelphia Merit Award – Built Category: 330 Cooper St.
Casualty: lecture and exhibition at Syracuse University
U of C Stony Island Student Housing

1120
CORNELL TEACHING DAIRY BARN
ITHACA, NY

CORNELL TEACHING DAIRY BARN
2009-2012

The teaching dairy at Cornell University was the first building of the Erdy McHenry master plan for the Large Animal Teaching Complex (LATC) which consolidates agriculture and animal facilities that were being displaced by the larger campus master plan initiatives aimed at increasing the density of the academic core. Our master plan effort needed to resolve the seemingly irreconcilable cross section of stakeholder interests, endemic to the academic and institutional client. The University Architect identified the dairy as a gateway structure because the site was situated off Dryden Road at the main access point for those coming to campus from the east. The College of Agriculture was concerned about their research fields which sit upland from the site and the College of Veterinary Medicine just wanted to replace their old dairy facility in the campus core which had been demolished. The lead veterinarian just wanted his cows to be happy, for reasons that are fundamental to the mission of a teaching dairy in a university setting.

There were two primary drivers behind the dairy facility program: it must model best practice strategies for a commercial dairy in upstate New York as part of the Cornell's Land Grant mission. The second driver, which forms the distinguishing characteristics of a teaching dairy, was to provide veterinary faculty, researchers, and students with an appropriately modeled environment to facilitate hands-on experiences on-site, as well as disease prevention, biosecurity and therapeutic intervention with individual animals and populations. For the herd, the increased level and unfamiliar character of exposure to humans in a teaching dairy is more intense and varied, ranging from multiple veterinary classes, to extension programs and even a handful of grade school class trips throughout the year.

The dairy anticipates these circumstances by including a bypass lane to facilitate staggered milking access to the parlor but also anticipating human traffic that allows visitors to be in the barn in a way that is less disruptive to the daily routine of the herd. The siting of the free stall barn orients itself to take advantage of prevailing winds to facilitate cross ventilation and combines with automated side curtains to maintain a comfortable and consistent temperature range for the lactating herd. The milking parlor is set askew to the barn itself in order to improve sightlines from a second floor classroom that allows classes and visitors a broader prospect over the facility and its operations. Perhaps the greatest evidence of accomplishment on this project was the fact that it was featured on the cover of Architectural Record and featured in Modern Farmer in the same month, corroborating the feedback from each individual university stakeholder that their issues had been fully addressed in the design solution executed for this challenging site and program.

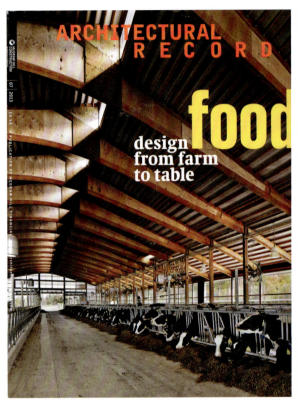

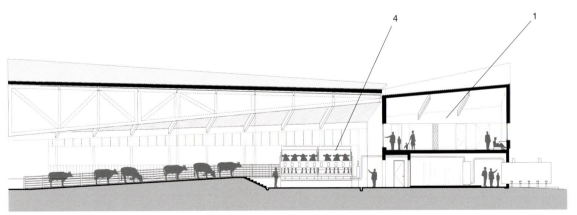

Diagrammatic Section

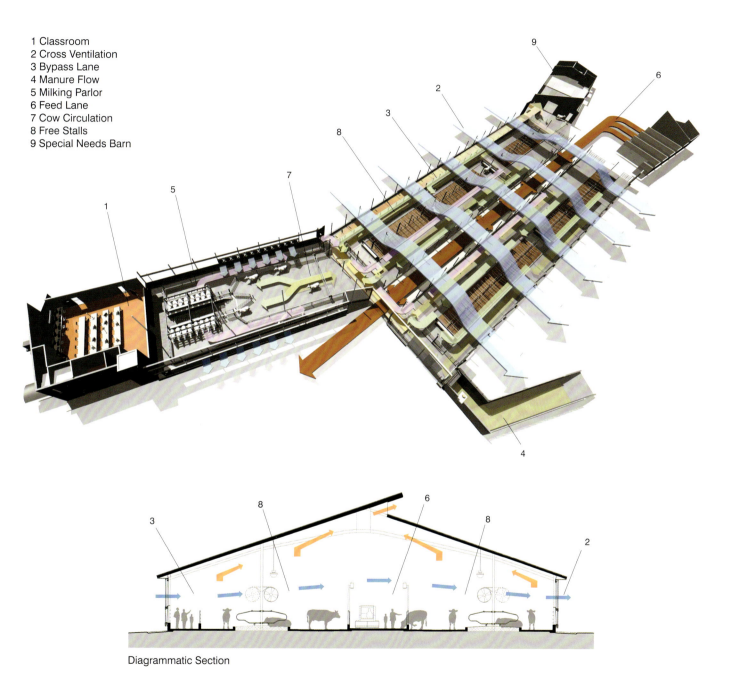

Diagrammatic Section

1001	Southern Poverty Law Center Headquarters
1002	Robinsons
1003	My Brother's Keeper
1004	Neptune Operations Center
1005	PS&S: Schools for Egypt
1006	NC Builders
1007	Comcast Graphics
1008	VGI Ops Pinnacle & LF
1009	Suburban Retail
1010	Prima Facie
1011	GI Ops Gallery
1012	Enterprise Center
1113	Walnut Street Lofts
1114	AIA Philadelphia Honor Award – Unbuilt Category: My Brother's Keeper
1115	AIA Philadelphia Recognition Award: Suburban Cable Retail Prototype
1116	AIA Pennsylvania Excellence in Design Unbuilt Category – Southern Poverty Law Center Headquarters
1117	Philadelphia Water Department, Office of Watersheds, Best Stormwater Management Practices: The Radian
	GBCA Construction Excellence Award: Best Design Built Project – Drexel University Residence Hall
	CRRC Jumping Block
1118	Bollerman Parkway Falls
	Parkway Corp 23rd & Market
	Vertical Screen: Warminster
	Michaels Development: Copper Housing
	Architectural Record – University Multifamily Housing: Fringe Benefits "featuring One Hancock Square"
	Architectural Record HUD Housing
	Philadelphia Inquirer "Changing Skyline – Adding Coffee to the Culture (Independence Mall Café)
	Lumen-Air House – "Syracuse – From The Ground Up"
	Open House
1119	Drexel Dining Terrace
	AIA National Housing Award: HUD Housing
	AIA Philadelphia Honor Award – Built Category: Independence Mall Café
	AIA Montgomery Alabama Chapter Honorable Mention: Southern Poverty Law Center
	DBIA Pennsylvania Tri-State Region Design-Build Project Award: Drexel University Race Street Residence Hall
	GBCA Construction Excellence Award: Best Design Built Project – Drexel University Residence Hall
	Cornell Teaching Dairy Barn
	Mariana Bracetti Academy
1120	**Syracuse Intermodal Trans. Center**
1121	
1122	Goldman Cafe District Signing
	Lights of Liberty
1123	Metal Architecture Magazine "Divine Dwelling"
	Synterra Pnrs Broad & Spring Garden
1124	330 Cooper Street – MDC – CCTA Rutgers Housing Camden
1125	Campus Living Villages
1126	SU Law College Housing (Campus West)
	Enterprise Center
	Fertile Ground Exhibition
	Mariana Bracetti Academy
1127	The New York Times: "From Abandoned Brewery to Piazza, Philly-Style" by Terri Pristin
	AIA Philadelphia Honor Award – Unbuilt Category: Lumen-Air House
	AIA Philadelphia Merit Award – Built Category: The Piazza at Schmidt's
	AIA Philadelphia Merit Award – Built Category: The Radian
	Metal Construction Association President's Award: Roofing: St. Aloysius of Gonzaga Church
	Metal Architecture Magazine, Metal Roofing Award, St. Aloysius Church, Jackson, NJ
	McGraw Hill Mid-Atlantic Construction Award of Merit Higher Education/Research: Drexel University Northside Dining Terrace
	McGraw Hill New York Construction's Best of 2009 Project of the Year/Worship: The Church of St. Aloysius – Drexel University Millennium Hall
	McGraw Hill New York Construction's Best of 2009 Judges' Award Best Architectural Design: The Church of St. Aloysius-Jackson, NJ
	GBCA Construction Excellence Award: Best Design Built Project Best Commercial Project Over $15 Million – The Radian
	Best Overall Design Build Project, PA Region – Drexel University Race Street Residence Hall
	Philadelphia Inquirer "City's Green Groundbreakers" (Firm Profile) by Inga Saffron
1128	University of the Arts
1129	PPMC M.O.B./Surgery Center
	Ministry & Liturgy "St. Aloysius: A Tent for a Pilgrim People " by G. Scott Shaffer
1130	Goldman – New York City
	Open House
1131	Railroad Museum of PA (DGS)
1132	East Baltimo Community School
1133	PennDesign Renovation (Stuart Weitzman School of Design)
	AIA Pennsylvania Architectural Excellence in Design Citation of Merit Award: The Radian
	GBCA Construction Excellence Award: Best Industrial/Institutional Project Under $15 Million – Drexel University Northside Dining Terrace
	GBCA Construction Excellence Award: Best Industrial/Institutional Project Under $15 Million – Drexel University Millennium Hall
	Eastern Pennsylvania & Delaware Chapter American Concrete Institute Grand Prize Award for Cast in Place: Millennium Hall Student Residence at Drexel University
1134	Drexel Learning Terrace (ICI)
	Delaware Valley Regional Planning Commission – Regional Land Use Program of the Year: The Piazza at Schmidt's Common
	Realen Convention Center Parking Study (1324-1338 Arch)
1135	Philadelphia Inquirer "Changing Skyline" vertical screen building offers bright ideas for cubicle slave: May 20, 2011: Inga Saffron
	Bucks County Courier Times "New Vertical Screen headquarters puts green on display" June 2011: Lisa Shoemaker DeBree Staff

INTERMODAL TRANSPORTATION CENTER
SYRACUSE, NY

INTERMODAL TRANSPORTATION CENTER
2014-2016

The Intermodal Transportation Center (ITC) project started out of a need for a parking lot and a bus stop on the site of the new Center of Excellence, but the client wanted it to be more. The facility was to "tell a story" about sustainable design, with a focus on demonstrating the best practices in stormwater management and to inform the neighborhood of this important work. The vision for the site was to be an arts and cultural destination, to become a model of development for future urban blocks and provide a central location for alternate and transitional means of transportation. The design team's challenge was to incorporate these features in a cohesive way that would integrate into and enhance the existing site and the new Center of Excellence.

Located in Syracuse, New York near the intersection of Routes 81 and 690, the ITC parking lot and pavilion reside at the southern edge of a 2.4-acre parcel sharing the lot with the recently completed Center of Excellence Building (CoE). As a complement to the CoE, the ITC provides a home for integrated transportation services for the federation of firms, organizations, and institutions at the CoE creating innovations that improve health, productivity, security, and sustainability in built and urban environments. The CoE facility provides laboratory, classroom, and office space, but counter to a traditional introverted nature of research labs, the Center of Excellence laboratories open themselves up to the surrounding city, with the ITC as a threshold between the community and the highly specialized work ongoing at the CoE.

A parking lot for 100 cars is anchored by a large detention basin to mitigate the stormwater run-off from within the site. Five parking spaces are designated for hybrid vehicles and another five are equipped with car chargers for electric vehicle re-charging. Solar Energy Collection is a major design feature of the ITC. Using Photovoltaic (PV) and Solar Thermal Energy (STE) collection systems, the project is designed to generate all of its own energy. Solar power monitoring will be displayed to the general public, showing current usage as well as power being generated. By adjusting orientation to changing sun angles, the adapting structure will visually demonstrate seasonal optimization. In winter, part of the collected solar energy will be utilized to temper the environmental conditions for transit riders waiting for the bus.

The ITC incorporates several environmental features that reduce energy consumption, mitigate stormwater runoff, and provide a tangible point of reference for other ecologically minded urban projects in Syracuse. The ITC collects site-generated stormwater run-off in a shallow basin that encourages evaporation as well as transpiration through its use of planting. A controlled outflow connects the basin to the city's combined storm sewer system. As designed, this system maintains stormwater outflow below pre-development rates.

330 COOPER STREET
2009-2012

The City of Camden was among the poorest communities in the nation, prompting the State of New Jersey to initiate a publicly financed economic-development tax-incentive program. Together with Rowan and Rutgers Universities, the program aimed to revitalize the city's downtown and stimulate multiple metrics of community stability. The far reaching scope included the fiscal health of local government, better public safety and schools, and investments in housing, parks, transportation, and business.

While working with Rutgers University to expand the law school and medical school in Camden, the State leveraged private investment to provide housing and bring life and activity back to the downtown after dark.

330 Cooper was the first of those private investments, including acquisition of the land to provide downtown apartments for graduate students drawn to the city by Rutgers' expanding enrollment.

The economic and programmatic objectives were clear as we embarked on this project. The voice that we brought to the conversation was aimed at sustaining the social infrastructure of a long-neglected community. In the mid-1800s, Cooper Street was one of Camden's most prestigious thoroughfares, lined with beautiful mansions, estates, and gardens.

By the late 20th century, its aspect had changed from quiet residential to predominantly institutional and commercial uses which, until recently, was dominated by vacant homes and crumbling infrastructure.

This project was developed to reflect upon this history and culture of this community. The 12-story building, housing about 350 students, adopts a stark industrial form to serve as a backdrop to a more intimately scaled streetscape with approximately 7,000 SF of retail space on the ground level and residential loft units above, consistent with the 19th-century use patterns.

Because access during construction was so constrained by a surface light rail line that traverses the entire street frontage of the site every 30 minutes, the design and execution of the building relied heavily on prefabricated components in the structure and skin, including a manufactured steel structure, precast concrete floor slabs and pre-glazed and unitized terra cotta panels.

The scale and mix of uses on the street re-establishes a language of community, greeting pedestrians and residents alike. Through innovative building practices the building continues a distinct neighborhood vernacular.

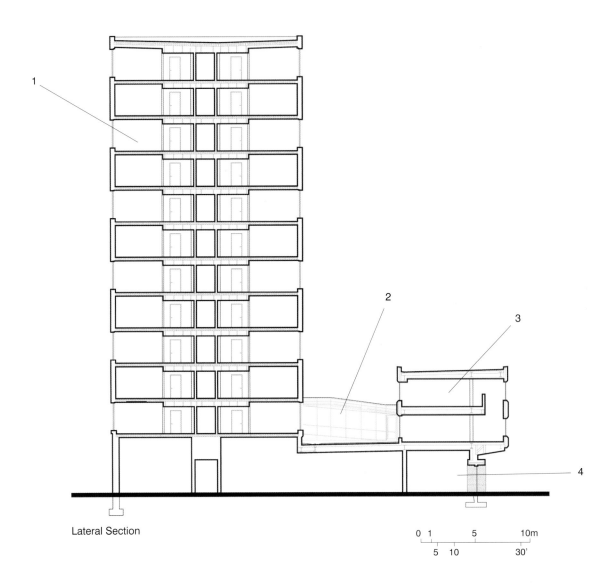

1126
SYRACUSE LAW COLLEGE HOUSING
SYRACUSE, NY

SYRACUSE LAW COLLEGE HOUSING
2011-2012

It seems that the sites made available by universities for development under public-private partnership agreements (P3) are often among the most challenging and least desirable for direct university execution. Shifting the challenges inherent in these sites to a development partner serves the University's interest and comports with the low risk-tolerance threshold among trustees and institutional governance systems.

An overflow parking lot on the edge of a steeply sloping embankment overlooking Interstate 81 in the shadows of the infamous Carrier Dome on the West Campus of Syracuse University was sufficiently challenged and thereby perfectly suited to this P3 development project. To make things more complex we learned that the proposed site was traversed over its length by a major underground utility line connecting to the campus cogeneration plant on the other side of I-81. Erdy McHenry Architecture, working with the Architect of Record, Holmes King Kallquist & Associates in Syracuse, NY designed this mixed-use housing for Syracuse University, specifically targeted to students at the Law College located on Campus West as well as other graduate students.

The site approach introduced a series of parterres to terrace the steep slopes in correlation to the definition of building height and the interpretation of what constitutes a "building story" in both the zoning ordinance and the applicable building code. In a similar way, the plan of the building utilizes a series of offsets in the footprint to negotiate between the rectilinear mandate of program efficiency and the incongruent path of the underlying utility easement.

The reconciliation of this complex geometry is expressed as an inter-connected, four-story wood-frame building following the contours of the site, in hill town fashion, enclosing an urban plaza with prospect over the interstate below, toward downtown Syracuse in the distance. The project houses 312 students in 191 apartments maintaining bed-bath parity across a mix of unit types from studios to four bedroom apartments covering a broad range of price points and demographics.

A coffee shop and convenience store located on the ground floor holds the street corner while a portion of the façade on Henry Street is pulled westward to create a series of public and private courtyards flanking the primary amenity spaces at the center of the facility, including a clubhouse with a fitness center, computer lab and business center, and a Department of Public Safety office. The planted entry plaza provides a forecourt to the building lobby and helps to modulate the block-long façade. Seating from the retail space on the south end of the plaza provides life to a long-dormant portion of Henry Street while an outside terrace on the western side of the main building lobby allows students a quieter setting for studies.

1133
UNIVERSITY OF PENNSYLVANIA
STUART WEITZMAN SCHOOL OF DESIGN
PHILADELPHIA, PA

UNIVERSITY OF PENNSYLVANIA STUART WEITZMAN SCHOOL OF DESIGN
2013-2017

The University of Pennsylvania, like so many other urban campuses went through a period of misguided planning in the '60s and '70s attempting to create an academic refuge apart from the streets of the city around it. With the recognition that academic institutions benefit from their physical context best by engaging with their host cities intellectually, socially, culturally and economically, the University of Pennsylvania has profoundly transformed itself and the city around it. This transformation is most evident in the revitalization of Walnut Street from the Schuylkill out to 40th Street and beyond, with one notable exception. Meyerson Hall occupies an enviable location both by virtue of its relationship to what is perceived as a primary "gateway" to the campus at 34th & Walnut Streets and its frontage on College Green and adjacency with Furness Library. Still it lingered for many years with its back to the street and the functional main entrance just behind the dumpsters. After an unsuccessful attempt to replace Meyerson with a new building befitting its prominent location, the School of Design and University Administration came to a shared consensus that a renovation and expansion strategy was the best option to make meaningful change in the foreseeable future.

Erdy McHenry was retained to create a master plan for the building, its program and its relationship to campus and the city. Correcting Meyerson's visual ambiguity and physical inaccessibility, while revitalizing its functional utility, was the fundamental impetus for transforming Penn's Graduate School of Design. The goals and objectives of the master plan establish Meyerson Hall as the center of design at the University by enhancing the quantity, quality, and efficiency of existing studio spaces. By consolidating research facilities, introducing designated critique space, and providing a place for informal academic discourse and interaction, the School of Design has worked to break down barriers between masters students, and encourage dialogue and collaboration across disciplines. Eliminating existing site barriers establishes an active connection along the busy west side of 34th Street, creating a cohesive urban edge. New windows introduced into Meyerson Hall enhance this street edge experience by exposing the interior creative activity to the surrounding campus. By eliminating site barriers and establishing a connection along the primary campus gateway, the overall site plan ties together Meyerson Hall and Frank Furness' Fisher Fine Arts Library to enhance connections to existing adjacent buildings, addressing issues of accessibility, visibility, and pedestrian flow.

A new, pronounced main entrance reorients Meyerson Hall toward the city and engages the campus edge to reinforce the high-traffic campus gateway at the corner of Walnut and 34th Street. Renovation of Meyerson commenced in 2013, and in the summers and winter breaks over the next five years the building was completely renovated including new and expanded studios and crit space, new classrooms, offices, fabrication shops, and most recently a new robotics lab. The main entrance was reoriented to Walnut Street while the MEP systems in the building were completely replaced. The last phase of the master plan is a major addition to the school, recently renamed the Stuart Weitzman School of Design.

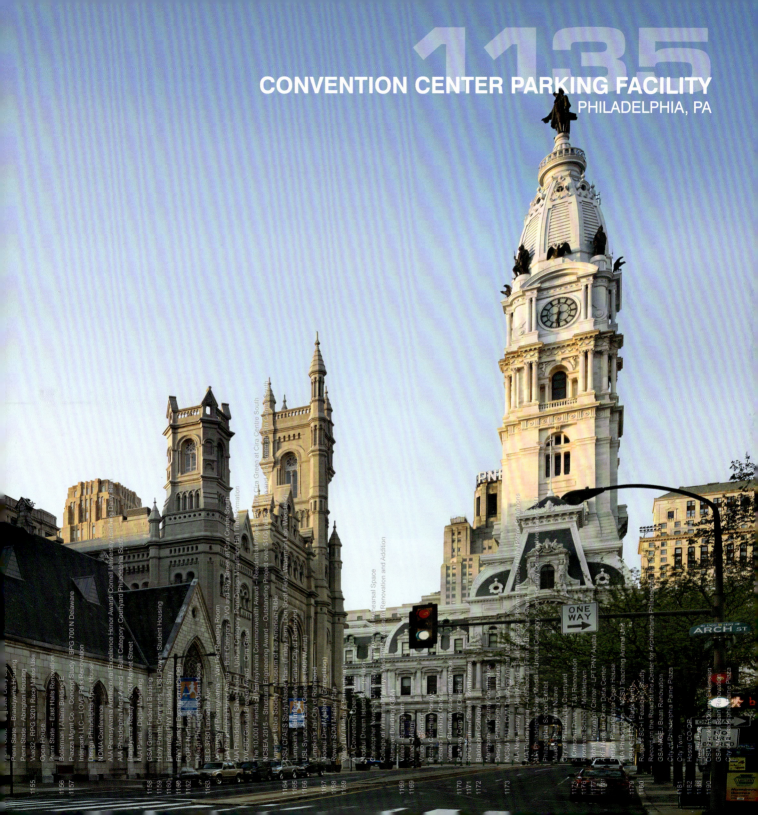

1135
CONVENTION CENTER PARKING FACILITY
PHILADELPHIA, PA

CONVENTION CENTER PARKING FACILITY
2010-2013

At the time of its completion, the Pennsylvania Convention Center's 1,000,000 SF of rentable space was the largest contiguous exhibit space and convention center in the heart of any American city.

With the expected influx of new conference-attendees and renewed investment in Center City Philadelphia, a vacant site, beholden to its unearned increment afforded by the convention center expansion just across the street, was predestined by the land owner to play a supporting role, providing convenient parking access for visitors of the convention center, adjacent office buildings and hotels. Left unconsidered, this ten-level, 540 car parking facility might have been content with the role of unfortunate secondary player, a necessary eyesore in the urban fabric. After our initial conversations and design proposals, however, the developer came to see the larger urban context and the community responsibility of any Center City building.

Beyond its purely functional and economic metrics, the proposed development of this vacant site was predisposed to interact with existing context and adjacency and to participate actively in the convention center neighborhood in ways that only arts and culture institutions seemed to embrace. Many factors about this sensitive location forced the project to be more than a concrete connection hub. The garage had to respond with sensitivity to the beloved architecture of the adjacent Arch Street United Methodist Church. At the heart of a bustling pedestrian district, the façade carried the responsibility of engaging the pedestrian experience at street level.

The upper garage is set back from the street line on Arch Street in deference to the corner tower of the church – a significant concession, considering the impact on the overall yield and efficiency of the upper parking decks. This articulation of the massing allows the corner stair turret of the 19th century gothic church to be visually complete from the street view.

Access control and revenue management functions of the garage are located at the second level in order to maximize the functional utility of the ground floor retail, both in the way that it engages the street and the service and loading requirements of the urban supermarket tenant that activates the street and services the neighborhood.

The upper facades of the garage acknowledge their urban proximity, using a pleated scrim of agricultural fabric and programmed lighting to put on a show for conventioneers otherwise consumed by their accumulating voicemails and text messages. An extensive green roof and attention to sustainable strategies help to reduce the environmental footprint of this facility over its useful life.

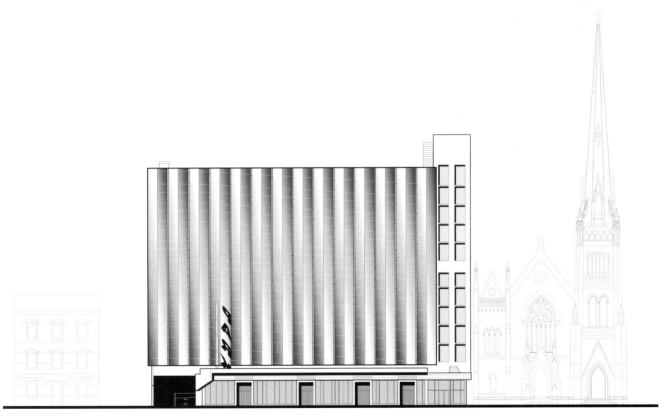

Arch Street Elevation

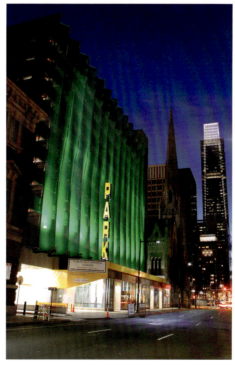

COURTYARD MARRIOTT AT THE PHILADELPHIA THE NAVY YARD
PHILADELPHIA, PA

COURTYARD MARRIOTT AT THE PHILADELPHIA NAVY YARD
2011-2014

The Courtyard Marriott is located in the heart of the Philadelphia Navy Yard, at a prominent location along Rouse Boulevard, visible from Interstate 95 and directly south of Center City Philadelphia. The five-story, LEED-certified hotel is a significant contributor in the continued revitalization of the Navy Yard and exemplifies Marriott's continuing efforts to advance larger sustainable design goals.

The project consists of a five-story, 172 room hotel, with an enhanced dining and bar/lounge amenity area, a fitness room for guests, and approximately 2,000 SF of conference space catering to burgeoning business interests at the Navy Yard. The design of the Navy Yard Marriott consists of a highly customized version of the traditional Courtyard Marriott brand. In response to the surrounding urban feel of the site, the building employs a façade system that animates its street-facing elevations, offering varying layers of color and shadow effects throughout the day.

The project is a unique, stand-alone exemplar of the Marriott brand that meets corporate branding requirements while offering visitors all of the quality and comfort that they have come to expect from the Courtyard brand. The hotel style is unlike any Courtyard Marriott in the United States; from the undulating façade panels to the continuous "ribbon" of the lobby and dining area to the custom designed furnishings of the guest rooms, the look is that of a sophisticated modern hotel one might expect in a Center City setting. This project illustrates the impact that progressive urban planning can have on a given typology as it is leveraged to redefine a national prototype. In this case, the prototype is the brand-standard Courtyard Marriott hotel, with design guidelines intended for a typical suburban site. At the Navy Yard, instead of situating the hotel behind a sea of parking as is typical in suburban locations, the building is pushed up against the main Navy Yard thoroughfare. Drop-off and porte-cochere are situated behind the building, along with parking, leaving the street-facing façade as a walkable environment with planted buffers between sidewalk and hotel. In the context of the Navy Yard Strategic Plan, a new social environment is emerging from the existing brownfields, encouraging pedestrian activity in lieu of the typical suburban auto-centric site design approach.

While the prototypical Courtyard by Marriott calls for business functions to front on busy main access streets, the Courtyard Philadelphia South employs an "urban mullet" strategy, placing the business side of the facility at the rear of the site near parking, and bringing the more active public spaces to the street and sidewalk. The building is pulled forward to maintain the street wall established by adjacent buildings with upper floors diagonal to the Central Green curve around the corner of Rouse Blvd and Intrepid Avenue in response to the landscape strategy developed in the park. At the ground floor, the building is notched inward to create an urban dining terrace that serves as an extension of the interior space.

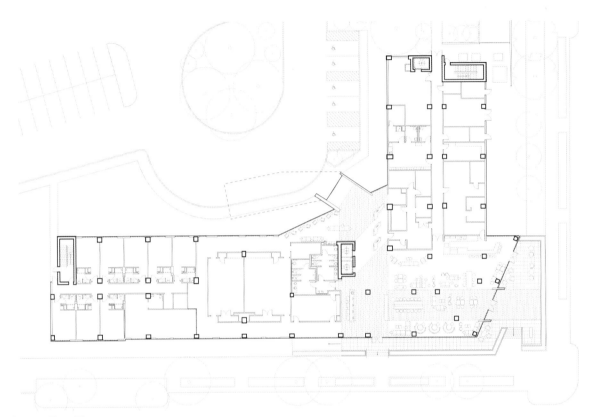

Ground Floor Plan

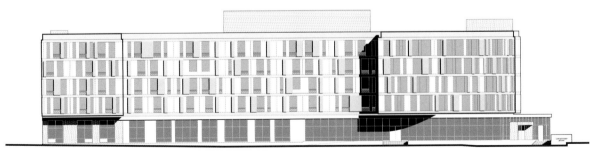

South Elevation

1 Steel Stud & Plank Structural System
2 Aluminum Rain Screen Panel
3 Hotel Amenity
4 Flood Mitigation Plinth

1120 AIA National Housing Award: NoLi Housing
1121 AIA Philadelphia Honor Award: Built Category: Independence Mall Café
1122 AIA Montgomery Alabama Chapter Honorable Mention: Southern Poverty Law Center
     DBA Pennsylvania Tri-State Region Design-Build Project Award: Drexel University Race Street Residence Hall
     GBCA Construction Excellence Award: Best Design Built Project – Drexel University Residence Hall
1123 Cornell Teaching Dairy Barn
     Syracuse Intermodal Trans. Center
1124 Goldman Cafe District Visioning
     Lights of Liberty
     Metal Architecture Magazine "Divine Dwelling"
1125 Sunterra Prins. Broad & Spring Garden
     330 Cooper Street – MDC - CCIA Rutgers Housing Camden
1126 Campus Living Villages
     SU Law College Housing (Campus West)
     Enterprise Center
1127 Fertile Ground Exhibition
     Mariana Bracetti Academy
     The New York Times "From Abandoned Brewery to Piazza, Philly Style" by Terri Pristin
     Ministry & Liturgy "St. Aloysius: A Tent for a Pilgrim People" by G. Scott Shaffer
     AIA Philadelphia Honor Award – Unbuilt Category: Lumen-Air House
     AIA Philadelphia Merit Award – Built Category: The Piazza at Schmidts
     AIA Philadelphia Merit Award – Built Category: The Radian
     Metal Construction Association President's Award: Roofing: St. Aloysius of Gonzaga Church
     Metal Architecture Magazine. Metal Roofing Award: St. Aloysius Church, Jackson, NJ
     McGraw Hill Mid-Atlantic Construction Award of Merit Higher Education/Research: Drexel University Millennium Hall, Philadelphia
     McGraw Hill New York Construction's Best of 2009 Judges Award: Best Architectural Design: Church of St. Aloysius—Jackson, N.J.
     McGraw Hill New York Construction's Best of 2009 Judges Award: Best Commercial Project: Over $15 Million – The Radian
     GBCA Construction Excellence Award: Best Design Built Project: Best Commercial Project: Over $15 Million – The Radian
     Best Overall Design Build Project, PA Region – Drexel University Race Street Residence Hall
     Philadelphia Inquirer "City's Green Groundbreakers" (Firm Profile) by Inga Saffron
1128 University of the Arts
1129 PPMC M.O.B./Surgery Center
1130 Goldman – Newark City
     Open House
1131 Railroad Museum of PA (DGS)
1132 East Baltimore Community School
1133 PennDesign Renovation (Stuart Weitzman School of Design)
1134 AIA Pennsylvania Architectural Excellence in Design Citation of Merit Award: The Radian
     GBCA Construction Excellence Award: Best Industrial/Institutional Project Under $15 Million – Drexel University Nesbitt College of Design
     GBCA Construction Excellence Award: Best Industrial/Institutional Project Under $15 Million – Drexel University Millennium Hall
     Eastern Pennsylvania & Delaware Chapter American Concrete Institute Grand Prize Award for Cast In Place, Multi-Possum Hall Structures: Millennium Hall
     Drexel Learning Terrace (CI)
1135 Delaware Valley Regional Planning Commission – Regional Land Use Project of the Year: The Piazza at Schmidts Commons
     Realen Convention Cent – Parking Facility (1424 – 1434 Arch)
     Philadelphia Inquirer "Changing Skyline: Vertical Screen building site to include store, May be Gallaries too" – Inga Saffron
     Bucks County Courier Times "New Vertical Screen Headquarters gets green light" by Crissa Shoemaker DeBree
     Beth Sholom Congregation
1136 LPT Commerce Center Bldg 3
1137 Courtyard Marriott / Ensemble Hotel Partners Navy Yard
1138 Brandywine Realty Trust
1139 LPT Great Valley Design Competition
     The 10,000 Friends of Pennsylvania Commonwealth Awards – Diamond Award for a Private Project – The Piazza at Schmidts
1140 Washington University in St. Louis
1141 Albany Medical Center (MDC)
1142 Evo Cira Centre South - Chestnut Tower
     Temple University Library
1143 Peak Campus Development – University of Chicago / Stony Island Site Student Housing
     Upenn Summer Studio
     Open House
     In Articulation-lecture at Temple
1144 AIA Philadelphia Merit Award – Built Category: 330 Cooper Street
     Casualty Lecture and exhibition at Syracuse University
     U of C Stony Island Student Housing
1145 Cira Skygreen – Cira South Garage Green Roof
     Penn Library Innovative Classroom
1146 UCD Social Seating
     Liberty Property Trust – Subaru North American Headquarters
     Brandywine – Queen Lane Site
1147 Architectural Record "The Cows Come Home" (Cover story)
     Campus Crest Communities
1148 Uncommon UVA – Campus Acquisitions Charlottesville
1149 Campus Acquisitions Morgantown WV
     Virginia Tech: Kentland Facilities
1150 PENN Medicine – PCAM South Tower
     AIA Central NY Citation for Design Residential, Multi-Family Project – Syracuse Law Campus Housing
     AIA Pennsylvania Gold Medal: Built Category: Cornell University Teaching Dairy Barn

1142
EVO & CIRA GREEN
PHILADELPHIA, PA

EVO & CIRA GREEN
2012-2014, 2013-2016

Philadelphia is a City of Neighborhoods that, at a variety of scales, establish community in a physical and social way based on individual responsibility, shared dreams, and common objectives. It is what William Penn referred to as a "Holy Experiment" where opportunistic mutuality and interdependence would foster a stronger and more sustainable community. It was a new way of living and a new way of thinking. Penn's concept did not envision the kind of density of today's urban centers but the principles are still operative at Philly's current urban scale. Evo and Cira Green literally stand Penn's experiment on its end. The same community-centric principles and social infrastructure that Penn envisioned as a sprawling "greene country town" are employed in this residential tower and Public Park, situated on the banks of the Schuylkill River straddling University City and Center City. In this vertical neighborhood, program and place are unified in a symbolic gesture reflecting the way that young professionals are transitioning from their academic pursuits to a world where community and social networking require physical interaction.

Evo is a mixed-use residential tower on the banks of the Schuylkill River developed in conjunction with Cira Green, a public park constructed atop an existing ten-story parking garage. The green oasis provides a respite from the urban condition all while demonstrating new ideas in blue and green roof technologies to manage stormwater volumes from the adjacent tower.

In the same way that Penn's public squares order the urban grid of Philadelphia, distributed amenities populate the program and the façade of Evo in a way that reveals the order of the community in a legible way both to the resident and to the broader public realm of the city at large. The amenity spaces are designed to accommodate quiet study, group collaboration and a variety of community interaction scenarios. These double height spaces are articulated on the building façade with an inverted "pleat" extending from the interior of the building. This "pleat" enables easterly views back to Center City and western views toward University City.

Cira Green establishes refuge from the congested streets below while offering the unique prospect of the city skyline. The building is designed to engage and inspire visitors and residents alike; large portions of the roof deck are tilted to facilitate distant views. A meadow in the center of the main lawn invites barefoot children to roll and romp in the grass and opens up to vast views of the skyline beyond. A terraced mound along the eastern parapet provides seating and intimate spaces for contemplation while sky gazing or enjoying the Schuylkill River waterfront.

At its inception Cira Center was an experiment in the same way that Penn referred to his plan for the city. With the completion of Cira Green, the Cira Center district of University City establishes the Schuylkill River as the new center of Philadelphia.

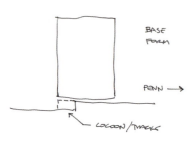
BASE FORM
PENN →
COCOON / TRACKS

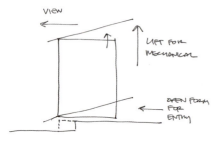
VIEW
LIFT FOR MECHANICAL
OPEN FORM FOR ENTRY

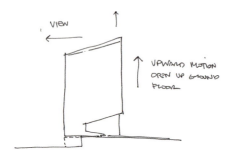
VIEW
UPWARD MOTION OPEN UP GROUND FLOOR

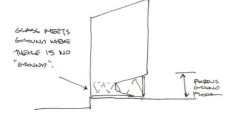
GLASS MEETS GROUND WHERE THERE IS NO "GROUND".
POROUS GROUND FLOOR

1 Rooftop Amenity And Pool
2 Double Height Social Space
3 Cira Green
4 Street Level Commercial

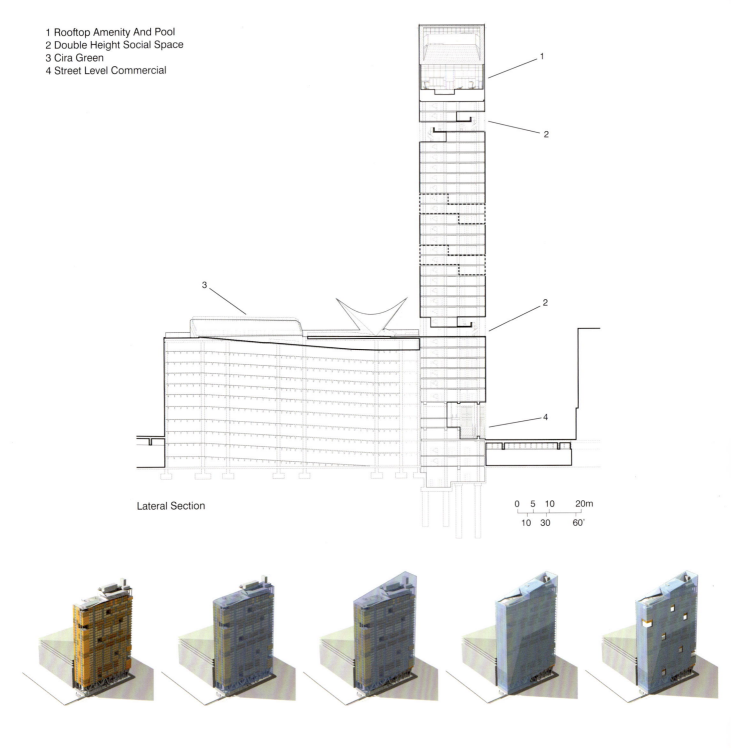

Lateral Section

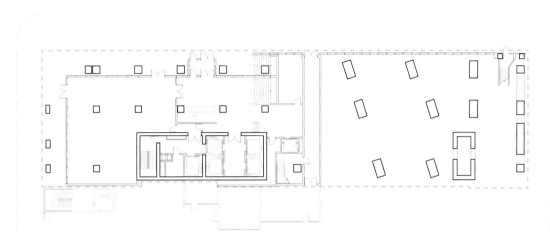

30th Street Lobby Floor Plan

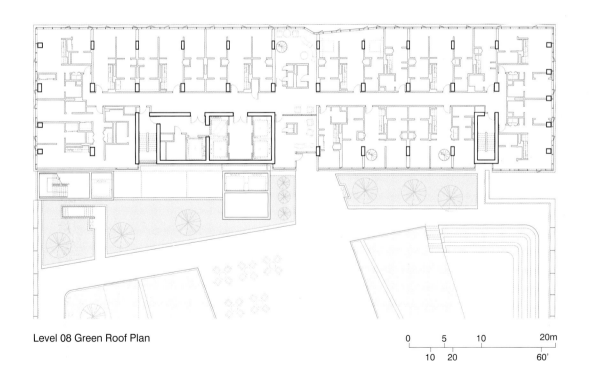

Level 08 Green Roof Plan

6 GREAT VALLEY PARKWAY
MALVERN, PA

The development of 6 Great Valley Parkway posits a new strategy for corporate campus planning and a building approach that focuses on the changing characteristics of today's workforce, allowing employees greater connection to one another in an urban styled campus, including connecting sidewalks, exterior shared spaces, collaborative spaces within, cafes, fitness, and green building performance to create an active, highly visible, energy-efficient landmark building.

The project rejects the traditional office block circulation diagram, using an expanded lobby to replace the traditional corridor and providing a centralized circulation radiating from an internal urban like setting that provides every tenant a physical connection to the central core. A daylit lobby stair connects all floors to the central lobby, encouraging users to climb stairs and meet, rather than ride elevators in isolation.

The building holds the street on the west side of the site, but exterior space was provided by pushing the building south, creating a small courtyard and terrace to provide tenants a venue for outdoor meetings and interaction. This front porch (1) connects directly with the interior collaboration area.

The skin of the building was conceived as a low-e glass box (2) enclosed by a composite metal rain-screen panel shroud (3). The entry locations are highlighted by notches in the metal shroud, exposing the glazed curtainwall system beneath.

A Collaborative Workspace was created where innovation is nurtured through informal, social, creative interactions. This combination of shifting employee expectations of group work experience and emerging company needs drives the design toward a variety of collaborative workspaces. The Central Gathering Space allows for casual interaction or company-wide meetings to take place, distributing ideas and information in both micro and macro scales.

As the client continues to replace the dated building stock of the office park, 6 Great Valley Parkway will serve as both a model and central beacon for all new office developments in the area.

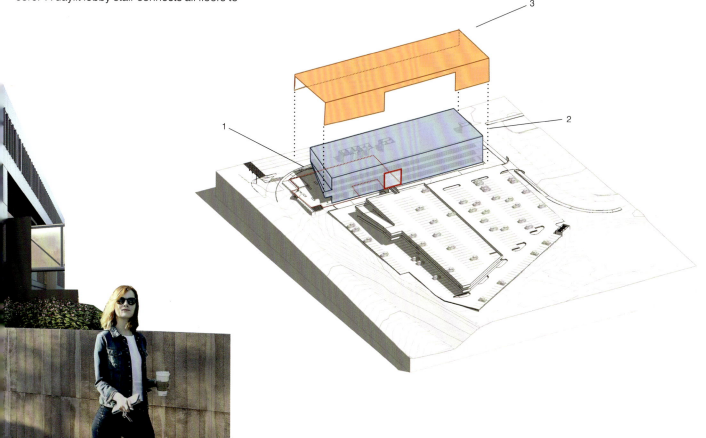

1154
WOODLANDS AT ARBORCREST
BLUE BELL, PA

WOODLANDS AT ARBORCREST
2014-2018

We have long been a disposable society. Throwing away a paper towel after a single use seems innocent enough, particularly compared to plastic trash bags, which we buy with the primary intent of throwing away. Still we have made great strides through conservation and recycling efforts to reduce the stream of waste that makes its way to the landfill. At first glance, we have made similar progress in reducing waste when we build new buildings, until you factor in building demolition.

According to the U.S. Environmental Protection Agency (2015), Construction and Demolition debris amounts to 548 million tons per year, or just about two-thirds of the solid waste stream in the U.S. with close to 90% of that being generated by building demolition alone. In other words, we generate twice as much waste from building demolition alone compared to the total generation of municipal solid waste.

How do we reverse that trend, particularly where the flight to quality among office tenants leaves an inventory of outdated and deteriorating assets in their wake? Even in a time when some suggest that bricks and mortar will yield to an increasingly virtual workplace, there is still an increasing demand for declining supply of quality office space, which fuels demand and causes rental rates to rise. The increase in rental rates drives the appetite for new development and the availability of funds to invest in real estate is almost insatiable.

This 1970's Pharmaceutical Headquarters building began life with a floor plate the size of six football fields. The original structure was fitted with tinted windows, giving the building a fortress-like appearance, reducing the amount of light and views available to the deep core of the building. Left vacant after a series of mergers and consolidations, this 203,048 SF three-story steel and brick fortress was slated for demolition and replacement.

Two fundamental interventions transformed the existing building into a modern and productive workplace. By removing an entire section of the middle of the building and installing a three story curtain wall, our team flooded the center of the building with natural daylight. New informal meeting venues and collaboration space were developed, available to all tenants. The lost square footage was replaced by repurposing the mechanical penthouse into usable office space that bridges the bifurcated segments of the three-story building below. The existing brick façade around the outer perimeter was retained and refitted with new windows.

The repositioning of this "sleeping giant" serves as a redevelopment template for countless underperforming assets across the country. Leveraging the embodied energy in the existing building to enhance the value proposition will only make any project better and might rescue marginal projects that otherwise might not pencil out.

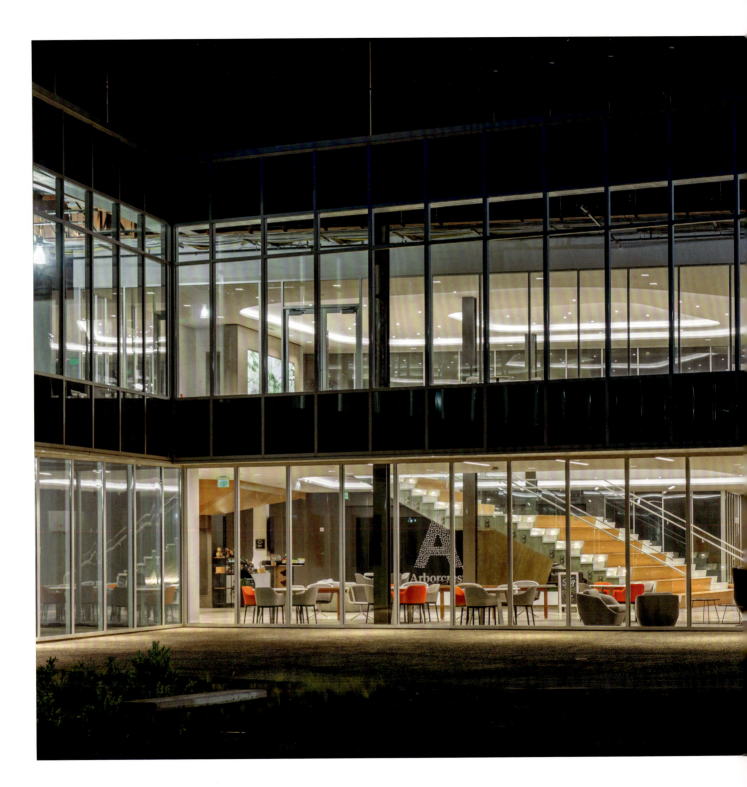

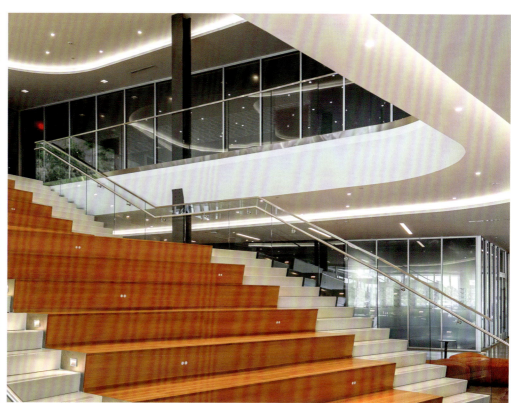

1118	Lumen-Air House - Syracuse - From The Ground Up
1119	Open House
	Drexel Dining Terrace
	AIA National Housing Award: NoJi Housing
	AIA Philadelphia Honor Award: Built Category: Independence Mall Café
	AIA Montgomery Alabama Chapter Honorable Mention: Southern Poverty Law Center
	DBIA Pennsylvania Tri-State Region Design-Build Project Award: Drexel University Race Street Residence Hall
	GBCA Construction Excellence Award: Best Design Built Project – Drexel University Residence Hall
1120	Cornell Teaching Dairy Barn
1121	Syracuse Intermodal Trans. Center
1122	Goldman Café District Visioning
	Lights of Liberty
	Metal Architecture Magazine - Divine Dwelling
1123	Sydney Grimm Bird & Spring Garden
	3rd Co-Gen Plant MDC - CCIA Rutgers/Austin Camden
1125	Campus Living Villages
1126	SU Law College Housing (Campus West)
	Enterprise Center
1127	Fall Spring Exhibition
	Marianna Brizzolli Academy
	The New York Times – From Abandoned Brewery to Piazza, Philly Style" by Terri Prister
	AIA Philadelphia Honor Award – Unbuilt Category: Lumen-Air House
	AIA Philadelphia Merit Award – Built Category: The Piazza at Schmidt's
	AIA Philadelphia Merit Award – Built Category: The Radian
	Metal Construction Association President's Award: Roofing: St. Aloysus of Gonzaga Church
	Metal Architecture Magazine, Metal Roofing Award, St. Aloysius Church, Jackson, NJ
	McGraw Hill Mid-Atlantic Construction Award of Merit Higher Education/Research: Drexel University Race Street Residence Hall
	McGraw Hill New York Construction's Best Project of the Year Worship: The Radian
	GBCA Construction Excellence Award: Best Design Built Project Best Commercial Project Under $15 million
	Best Overall Design Build Project PA Region – Drexel University Race Street Residence Hall
	Philadelphia Inquirer "It's Green Ground Breakers" (Firm Profile) by Inga Saffron
1128	University of the Arts
1129	PPMC M.O.B./Surgery Center
	Ministry & Liturgy "St. Aloysus, a Church of a Humble People," by G. Scott Shaffer
1130	Goldman - Newark City
1131	Railroad Museum of PA (DCS)
1132	East Baltimore Community School
1133	PennDesign Renovation (Stuart Weitzman School of Design)
	AIA Pennsylvania Architectural Excellence, Honorium Citation of Merit Award: The Radian
	GBCA Construction Excellence Award: Best Industrial/Institutional Project Under $15 million
	GBCA Construction Excellence Award: Best Industrial/Institutional Project Under $15 million
	Eastern Pennsylvania & Delaware Chapter American Concrete Institute Grand Prize
1134	Drexel Learning Terrace (CI)
	Delaware Valley Regional Planning Commission - Regional Land Use Program of the Year
1135	Realen Convention Center Parking Facility (1324-1338 Arch)
	Philadelphia Inquirer "Changing Skyline: Vertical Screen building offers bright ideas for display", 11/4/2011 Inga Saffron
	Bucks County Courier Times "New Vertical Screen headquarters puts green designs out front," by Crissa Shoemaker DeBreeStaff
	Beth Sholom Congregation
1136	LPT Commerce Center Bldg 3
1137	Courtyard Marriott – Ensemble Hotel Partners - Navy Yard
1138	Brandywine Realty Trust
1139	LPT Great Valley Design Competition
	The 10,000 Friends of Pennsylvania Commonwealth Awards: Diamond Award for a Built Project The Piazza at Schmidt's
1140	Washington University in St. Louis
1141	Albany Medical Center (MDC)
1142	Evo Cira Centre South - Chestnut Street
	Temple University Library
	Peak Campus Development - University of Chicago / Stony Island Site Student Housing
	Upenn Summer Studio
	Open House
	In Articulation - lecture at Temple
	AIA Philadelphia Merit Award – Built Category: 330 Cooper Street
	Casualty: lecture and exhibition at Syracuse University
1143	U of C Stony Island Student Housing
1144	Cira Skygreen - Cira South Garage Green Roof
1145	Penn Library Innovative Classroom
	UCD Social Seating
1146	Liberty Property Trust – Subaru North American Headquarters
	Brandywine - Queen Lane Site
	Architectural Record "The Cows Come Home" (Cover story)
1147	Campus Crest Communities
1148	Uncommon UVA - Campus Acquisitions Charlottesville
1149	Campus Acquisitions Morgantown WV
1150	Virginia Tech. Kentland Facilities

1159
HOLLY POINTE COMMONS
GLASSBORO, NJ

HOLLY POINTE COMMONS
2015-2016

A university education, more than simply the transfer of knowledge, encompasses a student's development of the intellectual, social, and personal skills needed to be successful in society. In particular, first-year student performance depends as much on their social and emotional adjustment to the demands and pressures of the university experience as it does on academic achievement. Developing new relationships in this unfamiliar territory is a critical factor in that transition, and the freshman housing experience plays a crucial role.

Understanding this social dynamic is key to understanding the "size" aspects of student housing ranging from the individual room to the suite, floor, building, and quad. In his research, British anthropologist and evolutionary psychologist, Robin Dunbar, discovered that the number of relationships that one person can maintain is limited, and the type and quality of these relationships vary by group size. As buildings, nodes, modules, and outdoor spaces are developed, we use "Dunbar's Number" to establish logical break points and clusters. These clusters can be identified as independent communities by the students. Smaller groupings of individuals will develop stronger bonds and consist of numbers ranging from 5-15-50, ending ultimately with a maximum community size of 150, where the members of the community recognize and are recognized by most all of its members. These living conditions, as a result, foment a productive and collaborative learning environment encouraging innovation and experimentation.

Holly Pointe Commons was developed in response to a request by Rowan University to work with their residential learning staff to develop a Freshman Village in part to accommodate an increasing enrollment profile but more importantly, recognizing the issues described above, to improve their freshman retention and success ratios. Located at the southeast corner of Rowan University's main campus, the site strategy creates a major new campus ellipse at the terminus of the existing pedestrian campus greenway which acts as a threshold between campus and community. Anchoring the western edge of the site, a new 550-seat dining facility overlooks historic Abbott's Pond. The new structure is surrounded by a rain garden serving as a visual/physical buffer and an environmentally responsible approach to stormwater management. The residential program is organized around communities of 35 to 40 students similar to a college house experience, providing for the physical and social needs of students. Social and academic development is nurtured and supported throughout the living/learning community by an integrated series of lounges, recreation facilities and laundry facilities encouraging interaction among residents. The facility is organized into 36 residential pods, each containing approximately 18 double occupancy rooms, one RA room, two single occupancy rooms, a common lounge and shared bathrooms. The building will also include apartments for the Resident Director and visiting scholars as well as Offices for management staff and office space for Rowan University Residential Learning & University Housing staff.

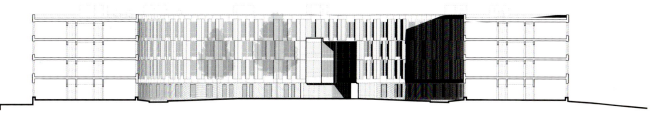

Southwest Section

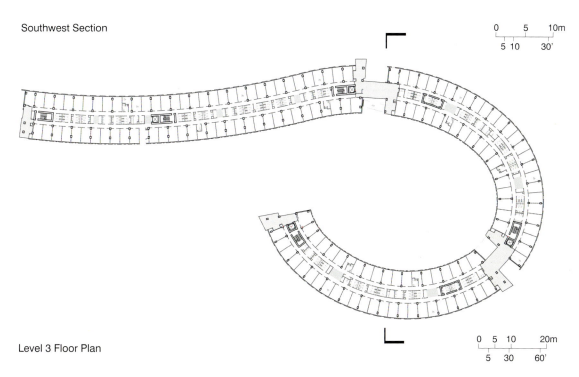

Level 3 Floor Plan

1 Green Promenade
2 Central Campus Axis
3 Pond and Retention
4 Green Space as Terminus

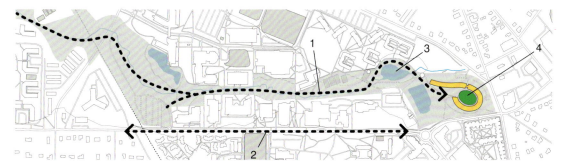

Campus Site Plan

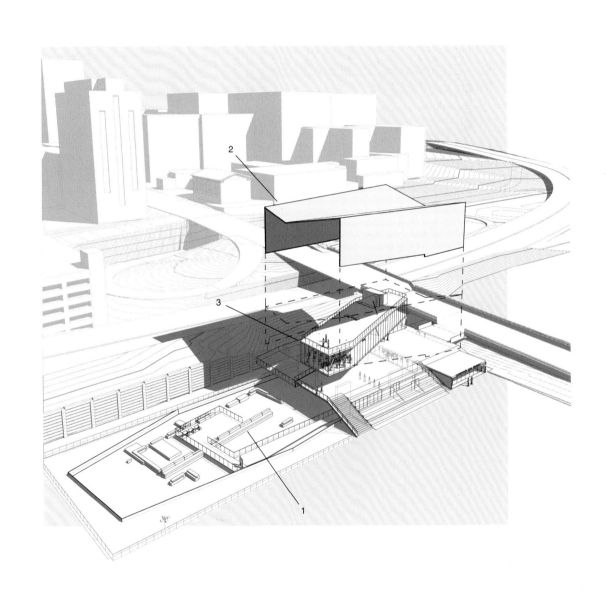

LUMPKIN'S JAIL INTERPRETIVE CENTER
RICHMOND, VA

The Lumpkin's Jail Interpretive Center sits along the Richmond Slave Trail, which commemorates the journeys of enslaved Africans. The trail tracks two journeys of enslaved people: the path from Africa to Virginia until 1775 and the path from Virginia to other locations in the Americas until 1865.

This concept for the Lumpkin's Jail Museum consists of two primary elements: the elevation of the pavilion structure to establish a prominence within the city of Richmond, and the exposition of the archaeological remains of Lumpkin's Jail (1). The pavilion housing the museum is designed to serve as the primary centerpiece between the Lumpkin's site and the African burial ground to the north of the site.

The floating and porous pavilion structure (2), constructed of corten steel draws references to the vernacular tobacco barns of slave-era Virginia, which represent the toil and oppression of the American slave. The interior of the typical tobacco barn provides a distinctive character when viewed from inside and out. This diaphanous texture is reinterpreted in the museum, as a delineating scrim that creates a sacred enclosure for the gathering space and the museum (3). The enclosure is elevated above the museum to provide sun shading for the interior while giving visibility to the museum from I-95 and downtown Richmond. The base of the pavilion is composed of a plinth of concrete stairs (4) creating a free and accessible vista of the historically significant sites. The main level of the museum is elevated above the archaeology of the slave jail, establishing clear sightlines from the museum and a more sacred relationship to the museum.

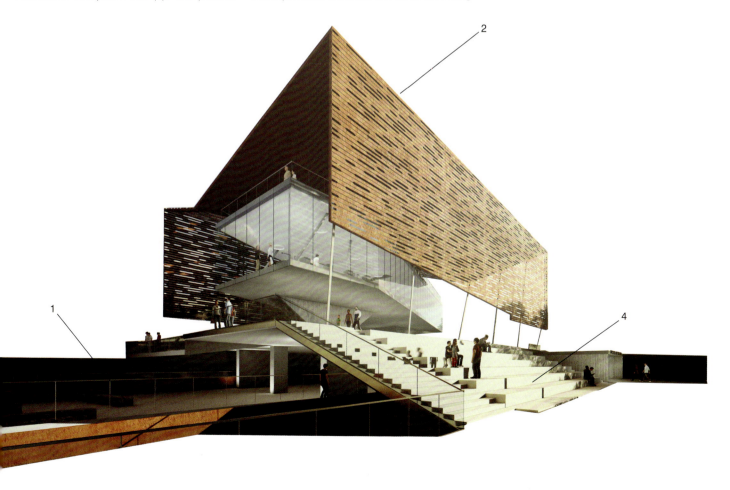

1177
AXALTA GLOBAL INNOVATION CENTER
PHILADELPHIA, PA

AXALTA GLOBAL INNOVATION CENTER
2015-2016

The Global Innovation Center for Axalta Coating Systems houses a high-bay R&D Pilot Plant with a two-story laboratory wing fronting on League Island Park in the Philadelphia Navy Yard. As industry continues to demand more environmentally compatible solutions, innovation and research are critical to Axalta's ability to develop the next generation of coatings and products. The facility will serve as the hub of the company's research and development program worldwide.

The building's particular location—at a crucial intersection of university research centers, office buildings, industrial facilities, future and existing hotels, and parks—imbue it with the responsibility to create a sense of neighborhood and energize key intersections of traffic. The main interior program elements of this 175,000 SF two-story R&D facility include business and professional offices, research and development laboratories, small batch manufacturing, and customer training.

The two-story loggia that runs the full length of 11th Street from Constitution to Kitty Hawk works in concert with Penn State at the Navy Yard to define League Island Park as a major public space conceived as part of the redevelopment master plan. Multi-trunk birch trees continue the rhythmic alignment of the street trees established in the Navy Yard masterplan. The street tree trenches act as a buffer zone between the pedestrian and the roadway, and have been designed to collect and treat stormwater runoff prior to reaching the roadway drainage system with stone filtration beds.

The front porch is reminiscent of the classically inspired buildings that were preserved in the adjacent historic core of the Navy Yard. As a threshold element between private and public, the colonnade frames and embraces the park with a two-story glass façade to maximize daylight in the workplace while utilizing the angled vanes that form the loggia to reduce glare and shade research staff from the low angles of the late afternoon sun. Parking is organized in the rear of the building in order to maintain the necessary urban edge and pedestrian oriented environment along 11th Street. The sweep of the building façade along Constitution Avenue. helps to screen the parking areas and creates a linear park connecting to the visitor entrance. By contrast, the Kitty Hawk façade takes its cues from the loft buildings and warehouse facilities common in the industrial district of the base. Neutral white façade elements stand in deference to the natural beauty of the park and submits to the deep ranging hues of the specialty coatings on display and visible through the scrim of the façade.

This industry leading research facility respects and celebrates both time and place in the way that Axalta's technology innovation continues the historical use of the Navy Yard while the building reinforces the historic expression of public space and heroic structures.

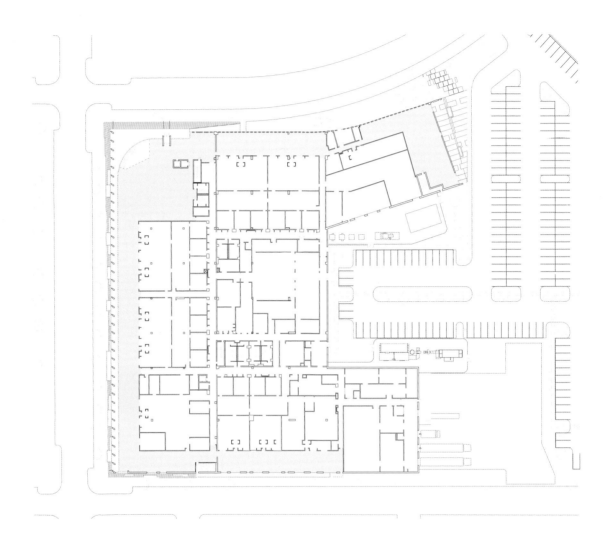

Ground Floor Plan

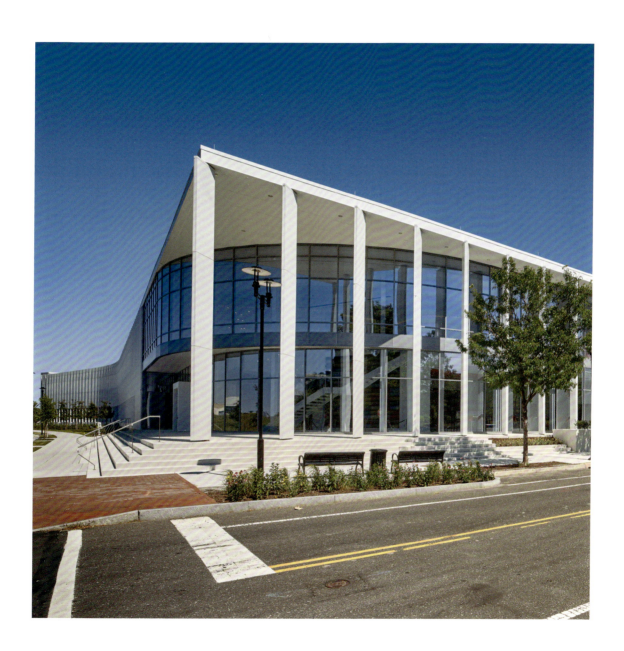

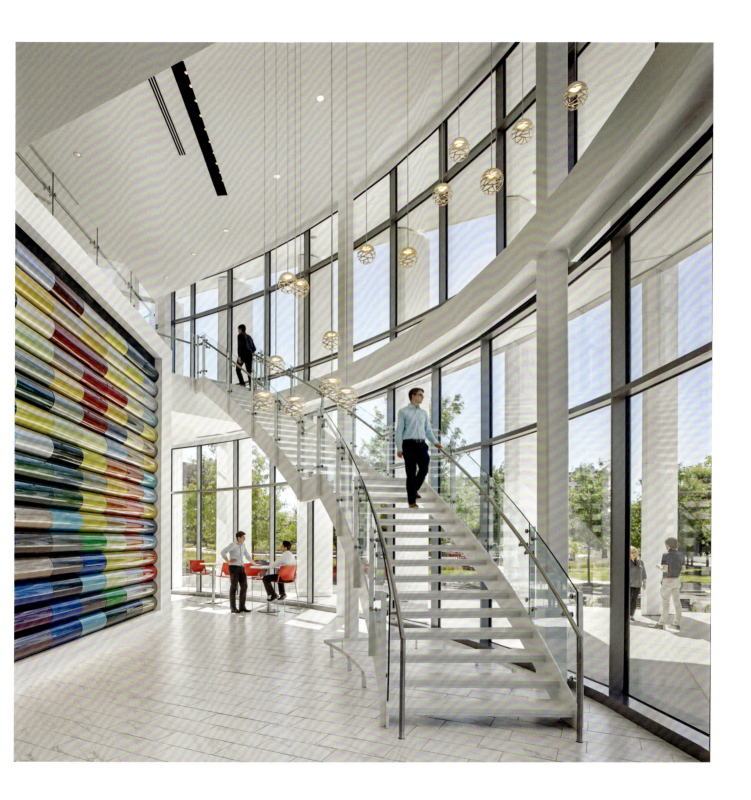

LIV BIRMINGHAM
BIRMINGHAM, UK

In response to food security issues facing cities worldwide, the tower brings the idea and process of farming to those with the most power to shape our future: the students of today.

This project, set in Great Britain's post-industrial city of Birmingham, is a bellwether project that addresses issues of food security whilst raising social consciousness of both local and global sustainability.

Growing food in urban areas eliminates the need for expensive transportation costs that raises both prices and CO2 emissions. Through measurable demonstration and engaged participation, this project provides both food and shelter for its inhabitants.

The building's façade (1), rendered in multiple shades of green-glazed terra cotta, draws upon an aerial imagery of Great Britain's agrarian past. In vivid contrast to the surrounding industrial context, the new residential building will be an oasis of color, drawing a clear synthetic distinction between urban and traditionally rural agricultural practices.

Built around a series of vertical farms (2), the mixed-use tower is designed to hold the largest educational community in the city of Birmingham, UK. Acting as both study space and greenhouse, these collaborative spaces (3) create a social community within the buildings that exposes residents to urban food security issues in various degrees based on their level of engagement. The building is an oasis for food-security research and innovation, pooling the resources of the local universities and the optimism of students to define a new model of apartment living.

By consolidating the young intellectuals from Birmingham City College, Ashton University, Birmingham Metropolitan College, and University of Birmingham, a new paradigm for living will be established. This next generation of world citizens will have the opportunity to learn first-hand the relationship between buildings and food (3) in their urban environment.

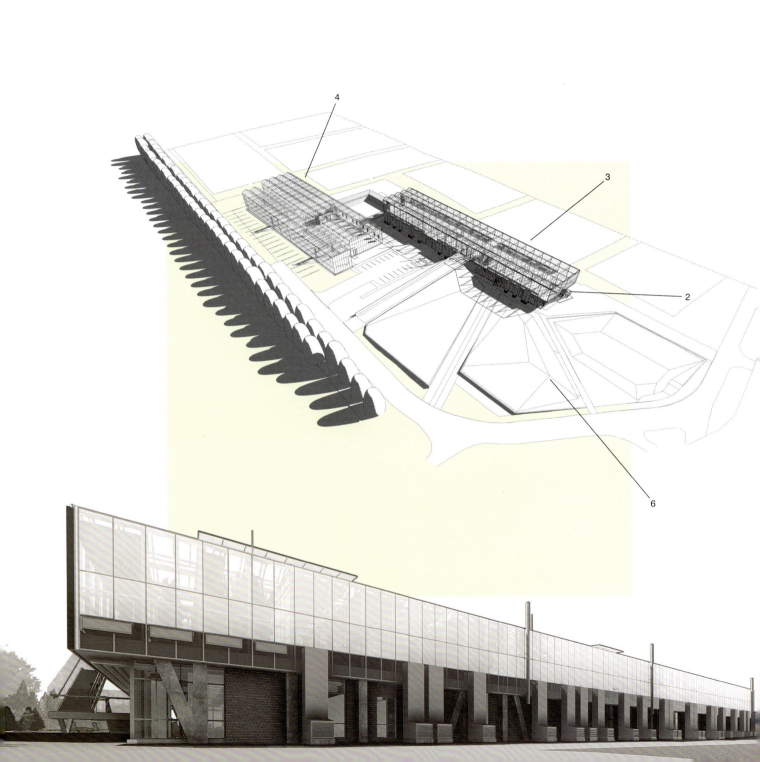

1179

BANK BARN
FRANKLIN COUNTY, OH

The Bank Barn is a state-of-the-art facility that provides interdisciplinary research opportunities for teaching, events, tours, and outreach programs, while increasing visibility of research associated with advanced methods of food production.

Surrounded by research fields, the facility is designed to celebrate both indoor and outdoor food production research. It is inspired by the massing of a traditional bank barn (1) and arranged to minimize its footprint on the site and accommodate future expansion possibilities. The facility includes a headhouse (2) and two main greenhouses, the Research Greenhouse (3) and Production Greenhouse (4). The Research Greenhouse is a five-meter Venlo greenhouse stacked above the headhouse and subdivided into small and medium sized compartments with unique internal environments. Stacking the greenhouse over the headhouse provides efficiencies in building footprint and utility distribution.

In contrast to the continuous glass enclosure of the greenhouses, the headhouse masonry envelope reads as a solid mass, with the exception of the main public spaces (5) which receive ample natural daylight and provide sweeping views of the surrounding site. Piping, ductwork, and conduit are predominantly exposed out of functionality and as a bold display of the building's working components. Typical greenhouse materials such as expanded metal mesh, galvanized steel, concrete and woven shade cloth reinforce the purpose of the building and work as a neutral background for the lush green color of interior and exterior vegetation.

Landscaped basins (6) define pedestrian paths leading to the building, manage the site stormwater, naturally filter fertigation waste water, and recharge groundwater. On the exterior of the building, a bank ramp provides people and small service vehicles direct access to the second floor of the Research Greenhouse.

5

1

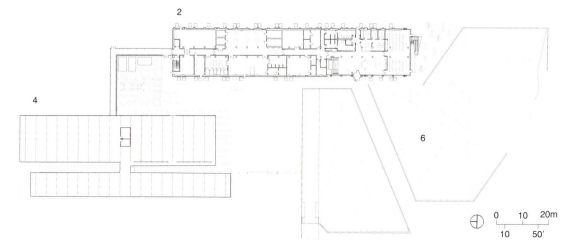

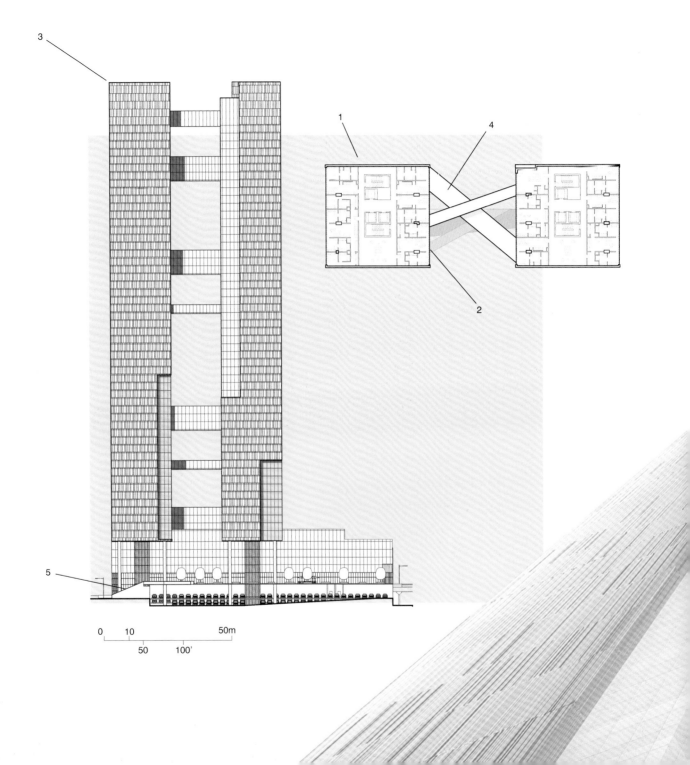

1181
CITY TWIN
PHILADELPHIA, PA

Located in a zero lot line condition, the residential towers are designed to maximize development potential of this large, deep mid-block lot. The zero lot line condition makes the placement of window openings problematic on facades directly facing the property lines of adjacent parcels. The proposed solution maximizes the development potential of the 480-foot x 80-foot lot by pushing solid walls out fully to the property lines (1) in order to maximize the footprint and appropriate the surrounding sky plane at the upper levels. Utilizing this strategy allows for fully glazed walls (2) to run perpendicular to the tangential views of the city skyline from the property.

The building is conceived as two separate towers (3) stitched together by bridges. The bridges (4) function as circulation between the towers, and are programmed to house the building amenity spaces. The towers are designed to sit lifted up off the ground level of the site, in order to accommodate a passage way (5) connecting an elevated 30th Street down to adjacent recreation fields at the neighboring Penn Park to the west of the site.

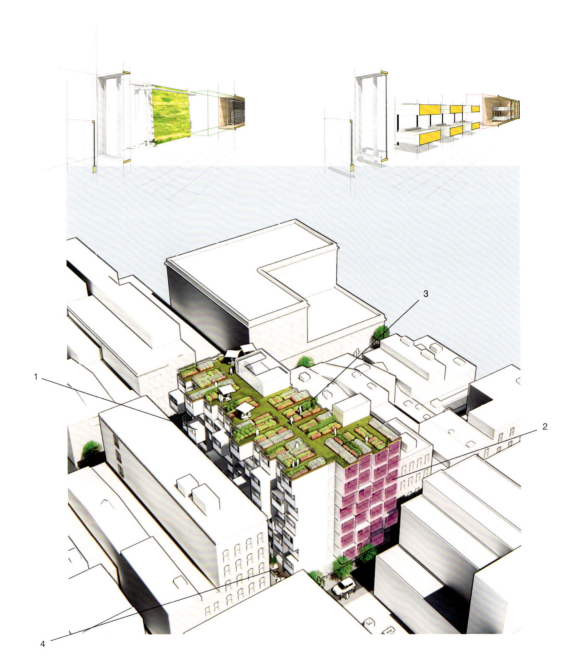

1182

HOSTEL COOP
PHILADELPHIA, PA

Food and shelter are basic individual human needs. Early hunter-gatherers were intimately involved in sourcing their own food and providing shelter for themselves. Early systems of agriculture set the stage for communal living around 10 or 11 BC with settlements in the Fertile Crescent. The decline of feudalism In the Middle Ages and the rise of cities and towns transformed the notion of community and moved agriculture from necessity to market opportunity. Today, our systems of food production and distribution have distanced food sourcing from the individual with a massive supply chain characterized by waste in the interest of efficiency. The same market focus on opportunity disproportionately impacts access by disadvantaged populations to healthy food, affordable housing and stable employment establishing self-sustaining barriers to the accumulation of community wealth.

The way that we approach urban planning and design can offer solutions to these inequities by creating a new type of architecture. One that is self-sufficient, provides employment opportunities and that allows us to reduce our physical and ecological footprint by living off the land and ultimately allows for a rewilding of an exhausted landscape now freed from the necessity of food production.

The COOP Hostel proposes a more affordable, cost efficient and sustainable housing that supports today's transient population while addressing the acute need for food security. Built out of carbon sequestering, prefabricated CLT units, the building combines hostel style housing with integrated agricultural production. Some units are set aside for at risk populations, others are rented as typical hostel accommodations (1). Each visitor participates in the growing process – some harvest vegetables in cutting edge Aeroponic grow boxes (2), while long term residents maintain their own plots of garden on the roof (3). The ground floor becomes a seasonal farmer's market offering surplus COOP-grown herbs and leafy greens (4). The building's modular construction allows for site specific configurations adaptable to empty lots across the urban landscape.

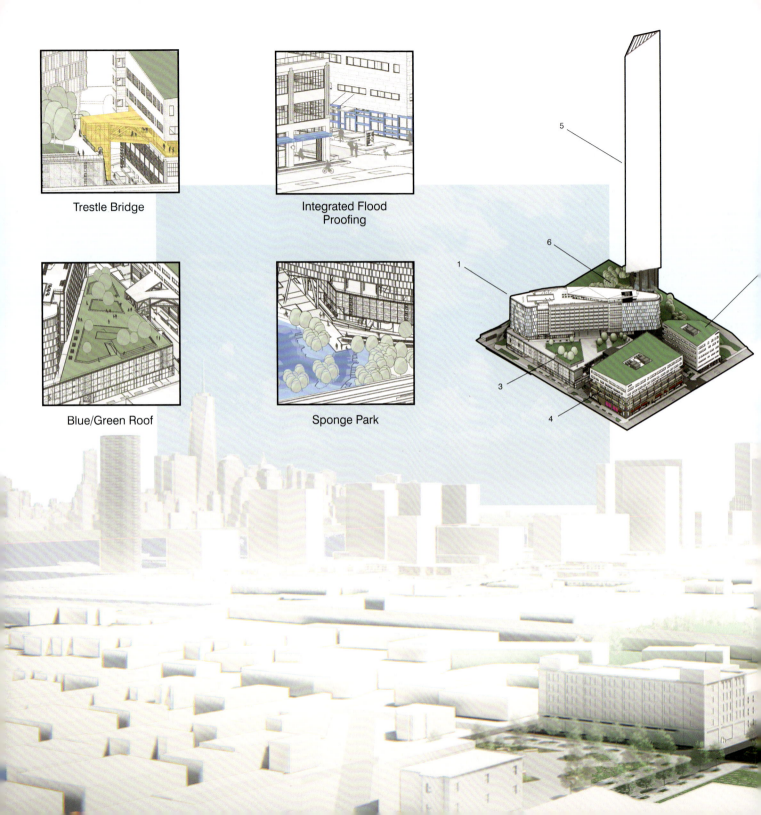

1188

TRESTLE PARK
HOBOKEN + JERSEY CITY, NJ

As an urban coastal city, Hoboken is particularly vulnerable to the effects of intense weather events that generate storm surges and flooding which pose a significant threat to life and property. Prior to Superstorm Sandy in 2012, this recurring threat had been met primarily with mitigation strategies and customary risk premiums to account for the economic effect but long ignored the environmental impact on natural resources and community health consequences.

The development strategy for Trestle Park confronts the environmental and ecological realities of climate change by embracing the architectural imperative to design in a more resilient way. In this context, every aspect of this master plan is informed by a programmatic requirement to anticipate, absorb, respond and ultimately recover when weather events impose their will on the man-made interventions that long ago disrupted the natural ecology of the wetland marshes between the Palisades Cliff and the Hudson River.

This transformative plan reimagines a former factory, its parking lots and an overgrown retention basin as a bustling and resilient destination district. The parking lot becomes a mixed use residential building (1) and medical office (2) whose parking garage supports an elevated park (3). A two-story overbuild on the old factory takes advantage of the latent structural capacity of its former use and enables the ground floor to be repurposed as retail spaces with office and event space on the floors above (4). Employees and guests can take the trestle bridge over to the elevated public park. The retention basin retains its initial function of stormwater overflow, but now in the guise of a resilient public park and the foundation of the residential tower (5). The minimal footprint allows the park to act as a recharge basin (6) that ebbs and flows with storm water events while maintaining public access year round.

Trestle Park will serve as a model for resilient adaptive reuse of urban industrial environments to ensure the future sustainability of our Cities

1190
FRANKLIN COUNTY EXTENSION
Columbus, Ohio

FRANKLIN COUNTY EXTENSION
2020

Waterman Agriculture and Natural Resources Laboratory Complex, home to many functions of the College of Food, Agricultural, and Environmental Sciences (CFAES), encompasses 260 acres on The Ohio State University main campus. Located just 5 miles outside of downtown Columbus, this site is unprecedented in comparison to other large urban campuses. The CFAES Master Plan embraces the idea of responsibly curating land use on Waterman and proposes several academic programs which serve that purpose. As part of those strategic objectives, Franklin County Extension acts as the threshold to the coveted Waterman site, bridging between the community and the University, consistent with its Land Grant mission.

The building has been sited to minimize disturbance to the surrounding fields and to align with adjacent agricultural structures. The ground has been lifted, rather than displaced by the building, to create an elevated green roof that camouflages the building from an aerial view, allowing it to blend into the surrounding crop and garden plots. The underside of the sloped roof is defined by the faceted wood ceiling on the interior. The terrain of the ceiling slopes up from the main entrance, reaching its highest point to the East where there are sweeping views of downtown Columbus and the surrounding farm. Staff areas and community spaces are coalesced under the unifying ceiling that makes no distinction between inside and outside nor public and private areas. Full-height glazing on the east and south façades underscore the connection to the land and to the constituent university and community stakeholders.

While the focus on practical agriculture remains central to the Franklin County Extension mission, the main emphasis of this new facility is to fulfill the needs of the youth and adults it serves. Each space in the building serves a purpose that focuses on a "learn by doing" mentality. In addition to gardening and cooking, the youth learn valuable lessons in leadership, communication, math, accounting, science, and technology. Large overhead doors allow community spaces to be utilized in multiple ways. The Lobby can become an overflow space for a large lecture in the Multipurpose Room or be closed off for a more formal event.

Waterman is situated in a recharge zone of the Olentangy River Watershed, a major tributary of the Scioto River. The green roof slopes to simulate the natural water flow by draining all rain water via a large scupper into a rain garden below. The rain garden was designed to accommodate a 100 year flood event and is used as a learning tool in sustainable practices for students and community members. This green infrastructure strategy ensures that rainwater undergoes phytoremediation in its progression over the building and its surrounding environment in order to protect the stream regeneration zone. With its careful site strategy, elegant and functional design, the Franklin County Extension gives legibility to the tangible connection between environment and pedagogy just as The Morrill Land-Grant Acts envisioned.

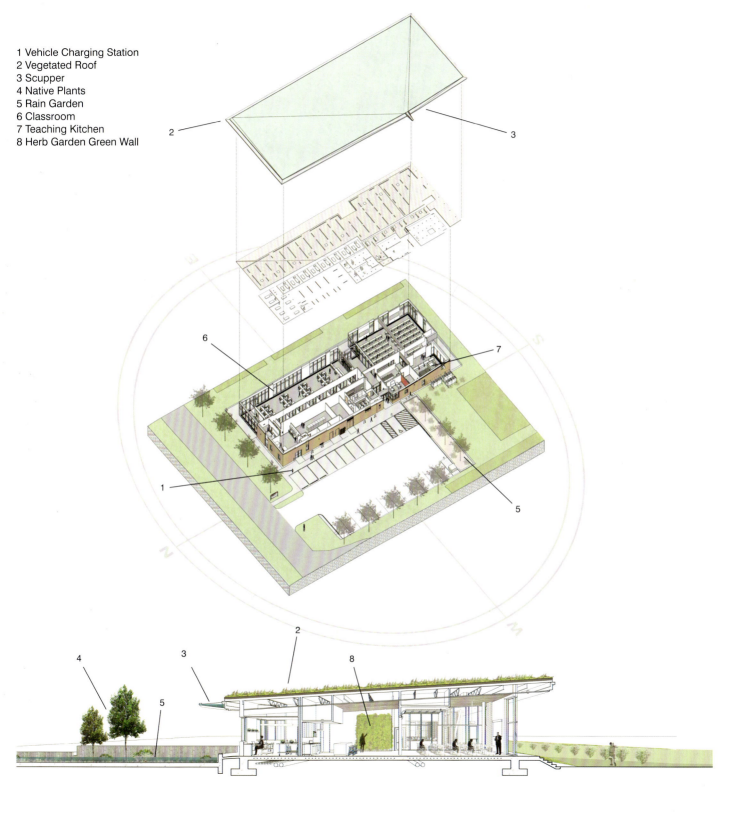

1192
NEPTUNE CAMPUS WEST
MALVERN, PA

NEPTUNE CAMPUS WEST
2017-2019

Public expectations of the financial services industry, and mutual funds in particular, prioritize accountability, reliability and responsiveness. This new building for one of the largest mutual funds in the world, the first new construction for them since the 2008 Global Financial Crisis, was in response to unprecedented growth in investment and pent up demand resulting from a conservative management perspective that eschewed significant capital investment in facilities development for almost 10 years. With more than 15,000 employees in the region spread across both owned and leased facilities, this assignment began with analysis of a changing workforce and evolving workplace norms aimed at accommodating a pressing need for additional space while at the same time testing strategies to reimagine more than 2.5 Million square feet of existing space to increase density, improve efficiency and optimize functional utility.

This company, owing to its conservative investment in the facilities development, had unwittingly widened a pre-existing gap between their current workplace and the expectations of an evolving workforce. The financial services industry found itself competing for workers with the tech sector in a market that had become more intense than ever. Holding onto talent once on-boarded had become equally challenging.

Curating an experience in the work setting begins with understanding the etiology of workplace evolution and an awareness of organizational structures and cultural norms. This new, four-story, 225,000 square foot facility was conceived through involved collaboration with our client. Our combined effort confronts this program of requirements in a way that responds to the immediate space need but also reimagines the workplace to be more flexible as it enables new solutions to future challenges and growth.

In this context, advocates for a strategic facilities plan were met by change agents grappling with the urgency of a pressing need. This type of scenario was examined by the noted academic and author on business and management, Henry Mintzberg; the focus on strategic planning was getting in the way of strategic thinking. One is analysis, and the other is synthesis. Understanding that the most successful strategies are visions, not plans, our effort focused on creating an environment for invention and exploration that would enable the workforce to discover the right combination of workplace elements suited to their mission and resources in support of the larger organizational objectives.

The specific placement of the new building is sited in a way it becomes a two-story 'bridge' connection between two existing buildings. The addition crosses main campus boulevard and creates an interstitial space of more flexible work stations and support amenities. The new incubator allows workplace innovation initiatives to be tested against the distinguishing characteristics of their established real estate infrastructure.

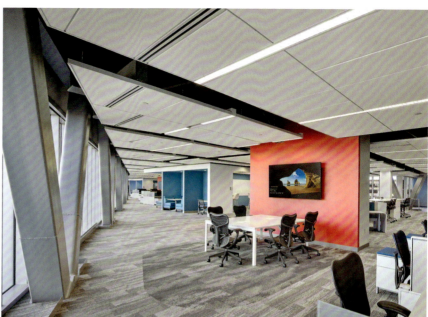

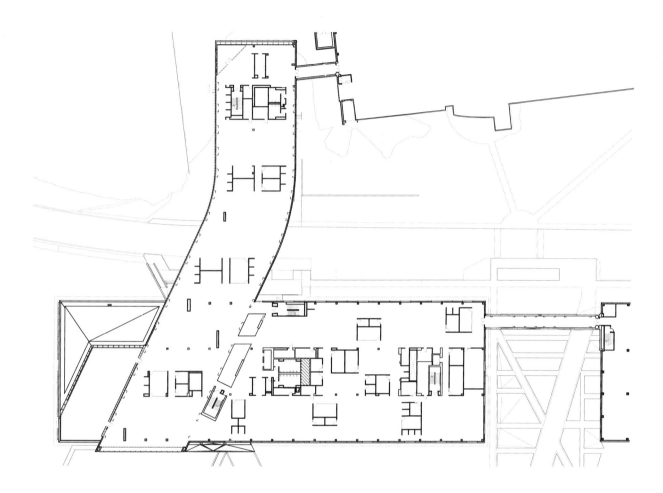

First Floor Plan

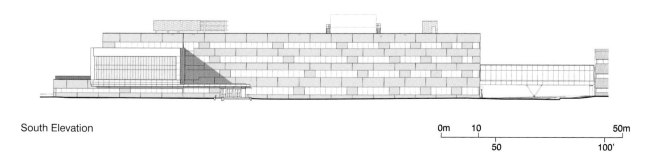

South Elevation

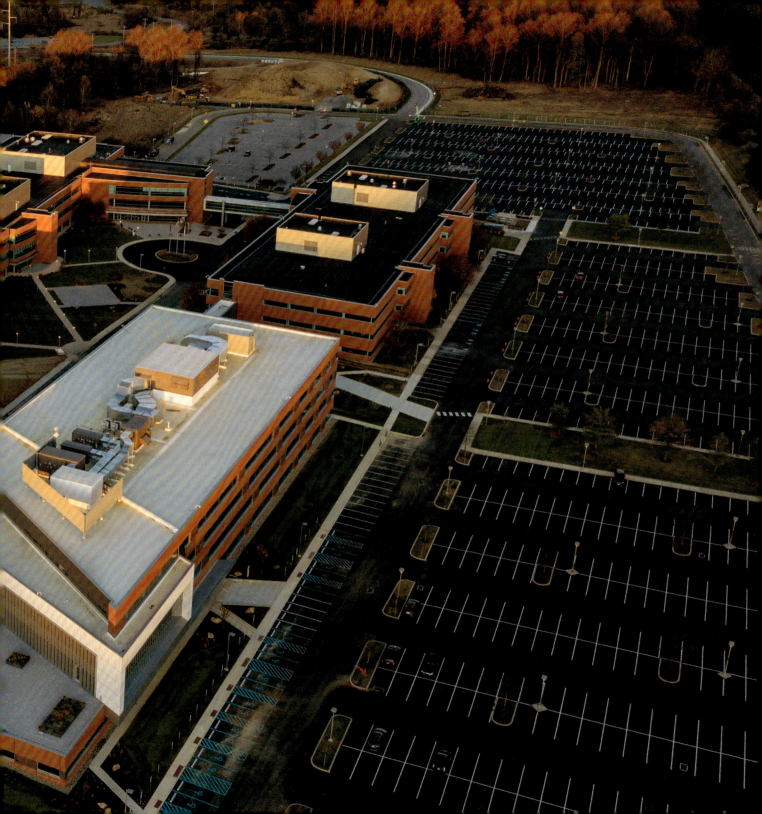

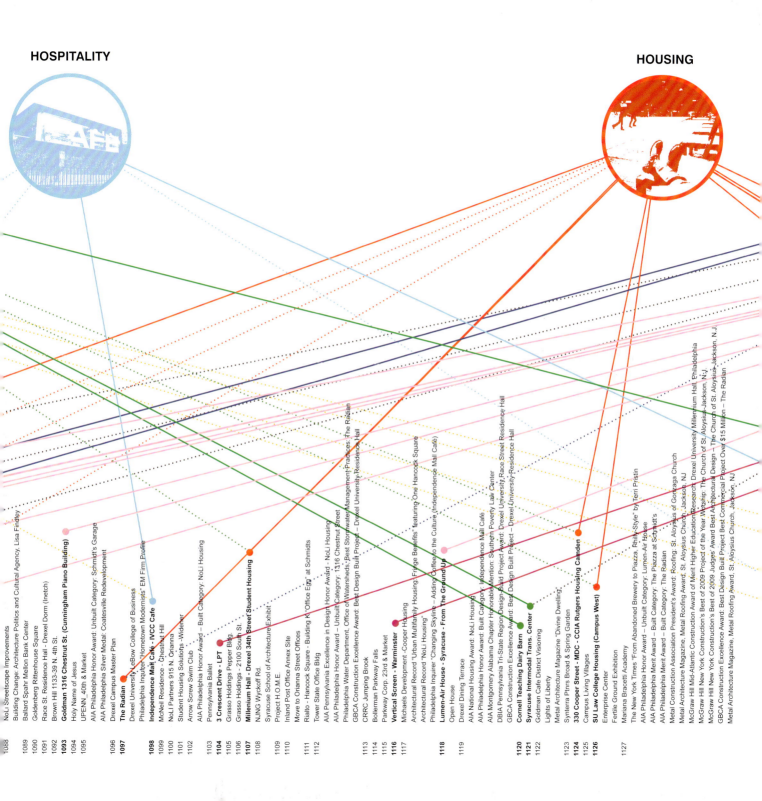

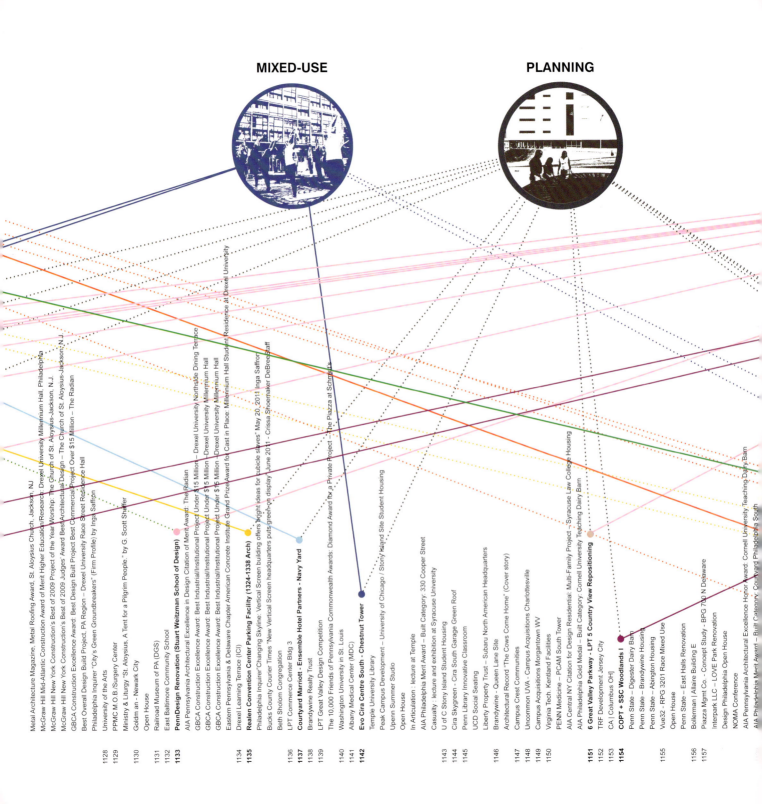

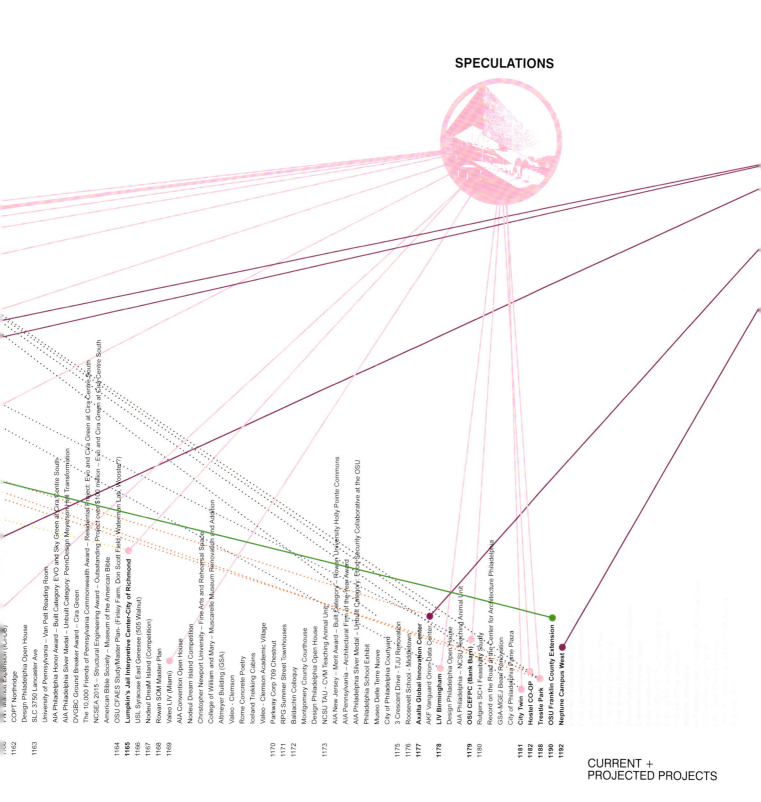

EPILOGUE
What's past is prologue

Throughout the last 20 years, it's been our privilege to participate in the project of the city. We bring to this discourse a deeply held belief that no place is placeless – it is emotional. The way we experience our surroundings brings into play context beyond the immediacy of tangible elements. In this interaction, architecture has the opportunity and the responsibility to engage with the user in ways we cannot anticipate as architects. It is part of our role as designers to understand each site, to come together with the community and stakeholders to learn and develop profound human spaces. We strive to create new opportunities for people to learn and participate in the urban environment with each building that we design.

Looking at our work in aggregate, we are aware that our practice has been impacted in direct proportion to and by the extent to which each project has contributed to the public realm and to the community it serves. Acknowledging design as more outcome than objective affirms for us that the shaping of our inquiry is a vital part of each solution. This methodology was a fundamental precept at the founding of the firm and becomes more refined with each engagement. In that sense, what's past is prologue, with a future still to be written.

A key challenge of architectural inquiry is the balance between utility and experience. The Cornell Dairy Barn, as an agricultural teaching facility, sits directly at this intersection of form and function. To build this project required a knowledge of agricultural systems and bovine social structure as well as commitment to preserving moments of human scale in a utilitarian space. In order to design successful, resilient, informed systems it is necessary to preserve what is beautiful about each site and project.

Probing the social and cultural infrastructure of place-making portends an approachable architecture. While the early Modernists introduced the benefits of efficient layouts and stark sculptural architecture to urban housing, it is a building's relationship to the surrounding context and history that determines success. The Piazza at Schmidt's does both. Inspired by the early Modernists, the building nests the bi-level units in a way that significantly reduced cost, while increasing opportunity for social interaction. The building creates a vibrant urban plaza merging into the fabric of the neighborhood. This move – pursuing both practical solutions and poetic architectural engagement – has long been a cornerstone of our practice.

When William Penn founded Philadelphia, he recognized that the inclusion of open space could help make his urban experiment more appealing to buyers. In doing so, he established urban green space as vital to the fabric of American cities. The need for and benefits of communal parks and orchards is only increasing as cities densify. On Cira Green, Penn's vision of the park is elevated above the parking garage and becomes a unique backdrop for picnics and wedding photos. Perhaps more importantly, it is a functioning component of blue/green infrastructure.

The interlacing of social, cultural and ecological intent highlighted in these examples gives way to a legible expression of purpose in the way we combine necessary resilient infrastructure with beautiful, city defining spaces. This is who we are, how we think and why we do what we do.

Shakespeare's use of the phrase "what's past is prologue" in Act 2 Scene 1 of The Tempest, on one hand suggests that all that has happened before establishes a predetermined, almost inevitable, path forward. A more optimistic interpretation and charge for the players is found in the context of the next line, "what to come, in yours and my discharge." In other words, everything up until now has merely set the stage for Antonio and Sebastian to make their own destinies. And so we too at Erdy McHenry Architecture look forward with optimism and renewed energy - excited about the future at yours and my discharge. Each project has opened more doors and made us better equipped to help our communities face the challenges of the next decade. We continue to believe that our investment in resilient and considered architecture pushes the project of the city forward to new possibilities. We design spaces where people forge new connections, where we learn and grow, where we are inspired to take on the challenges of the future.

Photography Credits

ARUP: 1107 Gordon Beall: 1116; Ray Cavicchio: 1154, Paul Drzal: 1071, 1107, 1142; Scott Erdy: 1034, 1107, 1116, 1121; Zamir Garcia: 1192; Goodwyn Mills & Cawood: 1001; Halkin Archictectural Photography: 1120, 1124; Halkin Architectural Photography (Architectural Record) 1120 ; Tommy Holt: 1097; Timothy Hursley: 1001, 1071, 1077; Christopher Kao / Philly by Drone: 1142; Peter Kubilus: 1071; 1097; Nicholas Mariakis: Introduction Image, 1003, 1097, 1098, 1104, 1107, 1137, 1142; Halkin Mason Photography: 1104, 1133, 1135, 1137, 1159, 1161; Don Pearse: 1154, Robert Pepple: 1126; Alan Schindler: 1034, 1104, 1116; Roger Swingle: 1077; Ann Tamutus: 1107; Roman Torres / Pixelcraft Inc.: 1034, 1098; Jeffrey Totaro: 1107; Albert Vecerka: 1142; Grenald Waldron: 1135

Collaboration

We are privileged to have collaborated on these projects with the following architects: Goodwyn, Mills and Cawood: 1001 Southern Poverty Law Center; Holmes King Kallquist & Associates: 1126 Syracuse Law College Housing; Arup/Cecil Balmond: 1107 Millenium Hall

Acknowledgments

Like many architecture firms, we are constantly confronted with a Janus paradox: faced with minute-to-minute problems to solve, we are pulled forward as we compete for new work and drive our design forward, just as we are pulled backward by our own success and precedent.

This book is at the intersection of these two competing influences. We recognize the incredible volume of work we have generated as a small firm in Philadelphia, just as we look ahead at what the next twenty years may bring.

As we look back through each project we are reminded of the people we worked with—so many of whom have been recurring partners, advocates, and allies.

To them we owe a great gratitude, firstly for their insight and expertise across so many projects and construction challenges, and secondly for their wisdom: the design feedback provided by subcontractors, owners, community members, and even our own friends and family, have constantly infused our work with renewed purpose and drive.

Most of all, we thank each of these people for their confidence in us and for their trust and partnership in bringing about the great works of architecture contained within this publication.

As professionals and educators, we would like to offer appreciation to the following colleagues of the firm throughout time, without whom the work in this book would not be possible:

Kevin Aires, Kristine Allouchery, Banu Ataman, Kristy Balliet, Katherine Banas, Nathan Barlett, Jose Barria, John Bastian, Mary Ryan Berzinsky, Christopher Boskey, Michael Brahler, Shannon Brennan, Alexandra Brinkman, Katy Brown, Sean Canty, Ilka Cassidy, Jane Cespuglio, Justin Coleman, Paul Coughlin, Angelina Dallago, Luke Dale, Robert Deacon, Anna Deeg, Raymond Demers, Grace Dickinson, Paul Drzal, Carl Emberger, Jacob Erdy, Mark Ericson, David Ettinger, Albert Fajardo, Nyasha Felder, Rosalind Foltz, Naomi Frangos, Zamir Garcia, Mark Gushanas Jr., Nathaniel Hammitt, Raven Hardison, Jason Harrell, Daniel Hawkins, Ryan Hill, Benjamin Hovland, Joseph Huang, Katie Stokien Hunter, Nam il Joe, Megan Johnson, Jordan Keller, Yair Keshet, Drew Kmetz, Aleksandra Kuzyk, Scott Larkin, Chang Lee, Kira Lehman, Ran Li, George Little, John LoVerde, Jennifer Mach, Elena Mangigian, Paul Marchese Jr., Nicholas Mariakis, John McHenry IV, Adelaide McInnis, Hana Mehta, William Metzger, Brendan Miller, Mark Miller, Jeffrey Mooney, Allison Morra Maxey, James Morrisey, David Niemiec, Eric Oskey, John Park, José Pertierra-Arrojo, Roshelle Pfeifer, Juan Pinto, Daniel Powell, Andrew Reilly, Julie Riley, Kyle Robinson, Carson Russell, Joohwan Seo, Melissa Shilling, Matthew Stachoni, Andres Stell, Patrick Stinger, Nathan Sunderhaus, Lois Soo Kyung Suh, Loren Supp, Olivia Tarricone, Angel Taylor, Jaclyn Thomforde, Patrick Till, Eric Torrens, Paul Trivellini, Susan Mackey Tunnicliffe, Emily Tyrer, Peter von Ahn, Ruo Wang, Yi Zhang, and Ashley Zimmerman.

Erdy McHenry Architecture
www.em-arc.com
215-925-7000
915 N Orianna St
Philadelphia, PA 19123

EDITIONS

Publishers of Architecture, Art, and Design
Gordon Goff: Publisher

www.oroeditions.com
info@oroeditions.com

Published by ORO Editions

Copyright © Erdy McHenry Architecture 2021
Text and Images © Erdy McHenry Architecture 2021

All rights reserved. No part of this book may be reproduced, stored in a retreival system, or transmitted in any form or by any means, including electronic, mechanical, photocopying of microfilming, recording, or otherwise (except that copying permitted by Sections 107 and 108 of the U.S. Copyright Law and except by reviewers for the public press) without written permission from the publisher.

You must not circulate this book in any other binding or cover and you must impose this same condition on any acquirer.

Graphic Design: Erdy McHenry Architecture; Scott Erdy, David McHenry, Zamir Garcia, Katie Stokien Hunter, Nate Hammitt, Al Fajardo, Nathan Barlett, Anna Deeg, Ashley Zimmerman, and Patrick Till
Text: Erdy McHenry Architecture and Nathaniel Popkin
ORO Project Coordinator: Kirby Anderson

10 9 8 7 6 5 4 3 2 1 First Edition

Library of Congress data available upon request. World Rights: Available

ISBN: 978-1-943532-62-9

Color Separations and Printing: ORO Group Ltd.
Printed in China.

International Distribution: www.oroeditions.com/distribution

ORO Editions makes a continuous effort to minimize the overall carbon footprint of its publications. As part of this goal, ORO Editions, in association with Global ReLeaf, arranges to plant trees to replace those used in the manufacturing of the paper produced for its books. Global ReLeaf is an international campaign run by American Forests, one of the world's oldest nonprofit conservation organizations. Global ReLeaf is American Forests' education and action program that helps individuals, organizations, agencies, and corporations improve the local and global environment by planting and caring for trees.